T0354978

EMOTIONAL INTELLIGENCE TRANSFORMATION

EMOTIONAL INTELLIGENCE TRANSFORMATION

DR. KIMBERLY PINCKNEY

EMOTIONAL INTELLIGENCE TRANSFORMATION

iUniverse books may be ordered through booksellers or by contacting:

iUniverse
1663 Liberty Drive
Bloomington, IN 47403
www.iuniverse.com
844-349-9409

Because of the dynamic nature of the Internet, any web addresses or links contained in this book may have changed since publication and may no longer be valid. The views expressed in this work are solely those of the author and do not necessarily reflect the views of the publisher, and the publisher hereby disclaims any responsibility for them.

Any people depicted in stock imagery provided by Getty Images are models, and such images are being used for illustrative purposes only.
Certain stock imagery © Getty Images.

ISBN: 978-1-6632-6824-2 (sc)
ISBN: 978-1-6632-6826-6 (hc)
ISBN: 978-1-6632-6825-9 (e)

Library of Congress Control Number: 2024922545

Print information available on the last page.

iUniverse rev. date: 10/29/2024

CONTENTS

PREFACE

I've always believed that true transformation begins from within. The journey toward emotional intelligence is deeply personal, yet its impact can extend far beyond individual growth – reaching into our relationships, careers, and communities. This belief, born from years of working with diverse groups, teaching psychology, and facilitating workshops, prompted me to write Emotional Intelligence Transformation. I wanted to create a guide that not only teaches emotional intelligence but also transforms lives, starting with our own.

This book is for anyone committed to personal growth- whether you're a professional seeking to enhance your leadership skills, a parent hoping to foster better communication with your children and family, or someone simply yearning for deeper, healthier connections. It's also for those who have experienced emotional hardship and are looking for practical tools for rebuilding trust and resilience, whether at home, work, or in social settings.

The reason I wrote this book is simple: I've seen firsthand how emotional intelligence can turn difficult situations around, restore broken relationships, and even heal long-standing wounds. My career in psychology, along with the personal challenges I've navigated, has shown me that emotional intelligence is not just a skill-it's a way of life. It's a path to understanding ourselves better, creating safer spaces for others, and ultimately leading more fulfilling lives.

Throughout these pages, you'll find insights, exercises, and reflections designed to help you develop empathy, manage emotional triggers, recognize toxic behaviors, and enhance your mental and physical well-being. But this book is not merely a collection of theories – it's an invitation. An invitation to engage deeply, reflect honestly, and take meaningful action toward lasting change.

I invite you to approach this book with curiosity and openness. Be willing to challenge your assumptions, explore your feelings, and embrace vulnerability. The goal isn't perfection - it's growth. And as you embark on this journey, remember: the changes you make today will shape your tomorrow.

Let's begin this transformation together.

ACKNOWLEDGMENTS

Writing Emotional Intelligence Transformation has been an incredible journey—one that would not have been possible without the support, encouragement, and inspiration of so many people in my life. First and foremost, I want to express my deepest gratitude to my amazing husband and two incredible daughters. Your unwavering support, patience, and belief in me have carried me through every step of this journey. Thank you for being my pillars of strength and for reminding me daily of the importance of emotional connection and love.

To the countless individuals I have had the privilege of teaching, working alongside, and mentoring throughout my career—your stories, resilience, and dedication to self-growth have inspired much of the work in this book. Every workshop, classroom discussion, and heartfelt conversation has deeply shaped my understanding of emotional intelligence. I am eternally grateful to have been part of your journeys, just as you have been part of mine.

I would also like to thank my colleagues and students at Chicago State University and National Louis University. Your intellectual curiosity and engagement have challenged me to think more deeply, and your contributions have been invaluable to my growth as both a student and a teacher, as well as an author. A special acknowledgment goes to the 100 men who participated in the research for my first book, When She's Mad. Your courage in sharing your experiences and your willingness to speak truthfully about the complex dynamics of emotional abuse have paved the way for a broader discussion on emotional intelligence transformation. You have helped shed light on a deeply important issue, and I am honored to have been entrusted with your stories.

To my editors, mentors, and the entire team that helped bring this book to life—thank you for your guidance, insights, and professionalism. Your support throughout this process has been invaluable. Finally, to the late psychologist Dr. Wayne Dyer, whose words continue to echo in my heart: "If you change the way you look at things, the things you look at change." This powerful quote has been a guiding force in both my personal and professional life, and I hope this book will serve as a tool to help others embrace this transformative mindset.

To everyone who reads Emotional Intelligence Transformation, thank you for embarking on this journey with me. My hope is that you find the insights, tools, and reflections in these pages to be meaningful, inspiring, and, above all, transformative.

With gratitude,
Kimberly Pinckney, Ph.D.

DEDICATION

To my amazing husband and two incredible daughters,

Your love, support, and belief in me have been the foundation of my strength. This book is a reflection of the love, resilience, and emotional intelligence we are growing through and sharing as a family. Thank you for always standing by my side and for inspiring me every day to grow, evolve, and transform.

To the countless individuals who have embarked on their own journeys of emotional growth and self-discovery,

May this book serve as a guide, a companion, and a source of empowerment as you continue to unlock your potential and transform your life.

To my mom and dad, you both have embarked and instilled in me love, trust, patience, honesty, and overall intelligence, and I truly miss and appreciate the love that you have shown me. I think of you both every single day.

And to everyone who seeks to change the way they look at things,

May you find that the things around you change in ways you never imagined.

With deep gratitude,
Kimberly Pinckney, Ph.D.
Thanks

ABOUT THE AUTHOR

Dr. Kimberly Pinckney is a seasoned educator, community psychologist, and advocate for emotional intelligence and behavioral change. With over 26 years of experience working for the State of Illinois and a robust academic background, Dr. Kim holds a master's degree in Human Development Psychology and a Ph.D. in Community Psychology, both from National Louis University. She has taught psychology at Chicago State University and National Louis University, specializing in courses such as Psychology 101, Social Psychology, Emotional Intelligence, and the History and Systems of Psychology.

Dr. Kim's first book, When She's Mad, was a groundbreaking research project exploring men's perceptions of women as perpetrators of emotional abuse. Using a mixed-method approach, she interviewed 100 men, offering deep insights into the often-overlooked dynamics of emotional abuse from a male perspective. This research set the stage for her continued work in emotional intelligence and behavioral transformation.

Throughout her career, Dr. Kim has hosted numerous workshops at HBCUs, the International Association of Women (IAW), and on radio programs such as "A Time for Inspiration" and the "AC Green Show." In addition, Dr. Kim assisted with the development of a curriculum through Adler University for a nonprofit organization, the Youth Peace Ambassadors Program, which focuses on emotional intelligence and empowering individuals to transform their lives through self-awareness and emotional growth. Her teaching and advocacy are rooted in her belief that true change begins with a shift in perception, guided by her favorite quote from the late Dr. Wayne Dyer: "If you change the way you look at things, the things around you will change."

Dr. Kim's latest book, Emotional Intelligence Transformation, offers further insights and tools for harnessing emotional intelligence to navigate life's challenges and unlock personal potential. She resides in Illinois with her amazing husband and is the proud mother of two incredible adult daughters. Dr. Kim continues to inspire change in her community and beyond through her writing, teaching, and advocacy.

CHAPTER 1

EMOTIONAL INTELLIGENCE

"In a very real sense we have two minds, one that thinks and one that feels"

— Daniel Goleman

Emotional Intelligence (EI) is a powerful tool for understanding people deeply. Often called 'Emotional Quotient' (EQ), it's all about recognizing and managing your own feelings and those of others. This includes skills like self-awareness, social skills, empathy, and the ability to compromise. Mastering these skills can greatly improve both your personal and professional lives.

Emotional intelligence is a game-changer for personal growth. It encourages you to look at your feelings and understand who you really are, including your strengths and areas where you can grow. By learning to recognize your emotional patterns and triggers, you can manage your reactions better and find more balance in your life.

EI also helps you connect more deeply with others. When you understand and empathize with other people's feelings, you can build stronger relationships, communicate more effectively, and handle conflicts in a more thoughtful and respectful way.

In the workplace, emotional intelligence is essential for career development. It influences how you lead, work with others, and perform your job. A leader with high EI supports their team, creates a positive work environment, and deals with conflicts well. EI also helps you navigate complex relationships at work, fostering teamwork and enhancing overall performance.

The concept of Emotional Intelligence became important as psychologists realized that just knowing facts wasn't enough to explain human behavior and success. Emotions play a big role in shaping how we think, act, and feel.

In the early 20th century, psychologist Edward Thorndike introduced the idea of "social intelligence" to highlight the importance of understanding and managing emotions in social situations. He showed how being emotionally skilled affects our ability to build and maintain relationships effectively.

Building on Thorndike's ideas, psychologist David Wechsler introduced the concept of "non-intellective" factors in the 1940s, acknowledging that intelligence encompasses more than just cognitive abilities. This shift paved the way for studying emotional intelligence as a distinct aspect of human intelligence.

The modern understanding of emotional intelligence gained momentum in the 1990s, largely due to psychologists Peter Salovey and John Mayer. They defined emotional intelligence as the ability to perceive, understand, manage, and use emotions effectively. This definition provided a framework for developing and improving emotional intelligence skills.

However, it was Daniel Goleman's 1995 book, **Emotional Intelligence: Why It Can Matter More Than IQ**, that brought emotional intelligence into the mainstream. Goleman's book combined scientific research, real-life stories, and practical insights to highlight the critical role of emotional intelligence in our lives. It became a bestseller, sparking widespread interest in the concept and its potential for personal and professional growth.

Since then, extensive research has explored various aspects of emotional intelligence and its impact on everyday issues. Studies have linked emotional intelligence to improved mental health, stronger relationships, enhanced leadership effectiveness, and overall well-being.

Emotional intelligence also helps us manage our emotions. It enables us to cope with anxiety, stress, frustration, and anger without letting these feelings negatively impact our decisions. By learning emotional self-control, we can handle challenging situations with composure and grace, maintaining inner balance even in difficult circumstances.

This emotional connection is crucial for building and nurturing relationships. It fosters trust and mutual understanding, creating an environment where individuals feel valued, heard, and supported, which leads to stronger personal and professional connections.

Emotional intelligence is useful in various contexts of daily life. Interpersonal relationships empower us to develop deeper influences with those we love, encouraging kindness and empathy. We may create happier and healthier relationships by being sensitive and accepting our friends, family, and partners' emotions. Emotional Intelligence surely helps us navigate conflicts and differences by facilitating effective communication. EI is greatly appreciated in the workplace. It enhances teamwork, leadership abilities, and general job performance. Emotionally intelligent leaders inspire and motivate their groups, fostering an atmosphere that fosters cooperation, creativity, and progress. They can understand and meet their employees' needs and create a supportive and upbeat work environment.

Beyond the personal and professional realms, emotional intelligence has a broader social impact and encourages understanding and empathy, fostering a more concerned and comprehensive society. A society that values EI is one where individuals celebrate and also respect diversity. Where conflicts are fixed with empathy and where collective well-being is focused.

Emotional intelligence is a lifetime journey to be developed that needs self-reflection, practice, and nonstop learning. Strategies such as self-awareness exercises, active listening and mindfulness practices, and looking for feedback from other people can contribute to the development. We can enhance our ability to resolve the complexities of everyday life, make wiser decisions, and eventually lead a more rewarding and meaningful existence by purifying our level of emotional intelligence.

Emotional intelligence is a complex set of skills that includes numerous components. It plays a key role in understanding and handling emotions efficiently. Self-awareness, self-regulation, empathy, and social skills can be gained by exploring the vital components of EI. Through this, we can better understand this transformative capacity and its impact on our personal and interpersonal lives.

Self-awareness is also an element of emotional intelligence. It includes the ability to diagnose and understand our own sentiments, thoughts, and behaviors without judgment. Self-awareness allows us to discover our emotional landscape, recognizing the tones, triggers, and patterns that form our practices. Through self awareness, we gain awareness of how our emotions affect our insights and interactions with others. This factor of emotional intelligence provides us with a solid initial point on the journey of self-discovery and personal growth.

Building upon self-awareness, self-regulation arises as a vital component of emotional intelligence. It demands the ability to achieve and channel our feelings in a positive way. Through self-regulation, we develop the ability to control impulsive responses, handle stress successfully, and maintain emotional stability. This element allows us to answer kindly rather than react impulsively, leading to more careful actions and improved decision-making. Handle the challenges of life with flexibility, calmness, and a greater sense of control over our sensitive responses by improving our self-regulation skills.

The final component of EI is social skills. Social skills encompass a variety of abilities that enable cooperative interpersonal interactions. It involves effective communication, active listening, dispute resolution, and collaboration. We build meaningful connections, build strong relationships, and easily navigate social dynamics by enhancing our social skills. Social skills enable us to express ourselves genuinely, adjust to various social contexts, and foster positive and productive environments. This factor of emotional intelligence empowers us to link with others on a profound level, collaborate effectively, and contribute to a more harmonious and broad society.

Through developing and understanding these important components of emotional intelligence, "self-awareness, self-regulation, empathy, and social skills," we reveal the potential for personal and interpersonal growth. Each component links with the others, forming an inclusive framework that enhances our emotional well-being and improves our interactions with others. By cultivating self-awareness, we gain the foundation to effectively regulate our emotions and navigate social dynamics with skill and grace.

In our capacity to appreciate people based on emotional intelligence, we develop a deeper comprehension of ourselves as well as other people, settle on additional informed choices, explore difficulties with strength, and make significant relationships. Through the investigation and incorporation of these parts, we unlock the extraordinary capability of the capacity to understand individuals on a deeper level, prompting a seriously satisfying and delightful life. This also signifies the fact that your feelings are straightforwardly connected to how you convey them. Working on your ability to appreciate anyone on a deeper level assures you that you will deal with your feelings better, which will assist you in rightly expressing and managing your emotions.

You know what? Life is loaded with difficulties, both big and small, that can test our flexibility and affect our general richness. At these times, the capacity to understand individuals on EI stands out as a significant tool that assists us in exploring challenges with grace and encourages important connections. We can deal with our feelings, relate to other people, and construct links that give pleasure and satisfaction to our lives by governing the force of the ability to understand anyone based on emotional intelligence. We can really deal with our feelings, relate to other people, and construct associations that give pleasure and satisfaction to our lives.

When confronted with life challenges, the act of appreciating people in these situations permits us to comprehend and control our own feelings. It begins with mindfulness, which is the ability to perceive and recognize our sentiments without judgment. Gain knowledge of what they mean for our viewpoints, ways of behaving, and dynamic cycles by tuning into our feelings. This mindfulness engages us to answer deliberately instead of responding rashly, empowering us to use wise judgment and even gain strength to withstand affliction.

When we talk about the impact of emotional intelligence on decision-making, it is noteworthy and complex at the same time. Emotional Intelligence considers practical compromise to be more significant when choices require agreement or joint effort. EI sparkles in high-pressure circumstances, assisting people with staying cool and making clear-headed choices. It cultivates a climate where creativity is energized.

This is particularly significant in the work environment, as feasible communication is the way to introduce yourself, your insight, and your skill to your team members, and it is the way to have the option to put forth a concentrated effort well in the working environment. Great relational abilities are also a way to make advantageous working associations with your partners.

Noticing and understanding your feelings is the initial step to having the option to actually communicate. By having the option to interpret and communicate these feelings really in your communications, you will turn out to be significantly more agreeable in speaking with your partners plainly and surely.

The ability to appreciate individuals on a deeper level likewise permits you to see and comprehend the feelings of your partners better, hence improving your responses to them. Numerous nonverbal signs are used in communication and also in the unlikely event that someone needs them. This is the ability to comprehend and understand others' struggles and challenges in terms of communication.

As we finish up this chapter, you're welcome to think about the fundamental understanding of the ability to appreciate anyone on a deeper level and the potential it holds for individual and expert development. The capacity to understand individuals on it. It isn't simply an idea that groundbreaking experience enables us to explore existence with more prominent mindfulness, compassion, and flexibility.

CHAPTER 2

UNDERSTANDING EMOTIONS

"Success is not the key to happiness. Happiness is the key to success. If you love what you are doing, you will be successful."

— Albert Schweitzer

How we feel affects our personal and work lives. Understanding emotions is important for getting along with others. Emotions are a natural part of being human. They influence how we think, act, and interact. However, knowing what someone else is feeling can be tricky.

At home, being able to understand our own feelings and those of loved ones is key to building good relationships. When we can sense how friends and family feel, it brings us closer together. We can better support each other when needed. Not getting emotions right can lead to fights and breakups.

For example, say your partner seems down and distant. If you think they just don't care about the relationship, you might act cold or start an argument. It will make things worse. But if you realize they feel overwhelmed and need your comfort, you can respond kindly to help ease their stress. This strengthens your bond.

At work, getting emotions right is also important. It affects how well we do our jobs and how happy we feel there. Many employers now want people with "emotional intelligence." That means understanding and handling feelings well.

Imagine you're a manager with team members. One regularly misses meetings and seems uninterested. Without finding the real reason, you may think they're lazy. But a respectful talk could reveal private issues or too much work stress. As their manager, you can then react empathetically to get things back on track.

Misreading emotions at work can still cause harm. Maybe a coworker's irritation seems like hostility to you. You may then get confrontational, too, damaging your relationship. Or a customer's worries may go unmet if you misjudge their feelings, risking future business.

The aim is to make interactions at home and in the workplace smoother by better grasping how people feel. It takes effort, but it pays off in stronger ties and job success.

Understanding feelings well takes work in many ways. It involves self-reflection, listening skills, and noticing body language and social cues. You must also be open to feedback, think about your reactions, and keep learning.

One approach is journaling or mindfulness. Taking time to think about your emotions helps you recognize what you're feeling and why. It gives insight into yourself and how your feelings affect your behavior.

Also important is trying to understand others. Ask questions, listen closely, and stay open-minded to different views. Showing empathy and interest in others' experiences improves how you handle relationships and socializing.

Having strong emotional skills serves you well both personally and professionally. You form stronger bonds and deal with challenges smoothly. Overall, increasing your emotional intelligence leads to more fulfilling connections and satisfaction in life.

Getting your feelings right matters a lot. Misreading emotions can result in wrong actions that damage ties, personal growth, and careers. One example is in relationships at home.

Imagine your partner comes home stressed from work but seems distant. Seeing that as disinterest or annoyance could make you defensive or start an argument. This escalates things. However, they may simply need quiet time to relax. By opening up dialogue and figuring out how they really feel, you can offer helpful support instead of making assumptions.

Misreading at work can also backfire. Perhaps a client voiced worry over a project. Viewing their tone as hostile rather than anxious could make you abrupt in your response. This angers the client and threatens your business partnership. Taking a breath and recognizing their real emotions allows for addressing concerns with care and saving the relationship.

The bottom line is that understanding feelings accurately prevents mistaken reactions from harming important connections both personally and professionally. Prioritizing emotional awareness serves relationships, well-being, and achievement well in the long run.

Misreading our own emotions can also hold us back personally. When we don't realize how we truly feel, it's hard to handle those feelings well or share them with others. It creates a divide between what's inside and how we act, which feels weird and makes problems harder to solve.

For example, say you have a work presentation coming up and feel anxious. But you tell yourself you're "fine" and try to power through it without dealing with the anxiety. Ignoring your nerves may result in a subpar performance. Or the anxiety could distract you during the talk. However, facing your anxiety by using relaxation or asking colleagues for support leads to a smoother, more successful experience.

Understanding feelings accurately takes a multi-step process. First, self-awareness is key—noticing your emotions and what triggers them. Journaling or talking to a counselor helps gain insight.

Active listening skills and empathy for others are also important. Really trying to understand how other people feel lets you respond to them with care, offering help as needed. This makes socializing go more smoothly.

Other strategies include mindfulness, which gives a clearer perspective on thoughts and feelings. Getting honest feedback from trusted friends and family also provides a helpful outside view of how your emotions are seen by others.

Having strong emotional skills has many benefits. In relationships, it helps you support loved ones better. It improves communication, teamwork, and your perception of yourself as a valuable colleague at work. Overall well-being is also boosted as you learn to handle stress, gain resilience, and maintain positivity. When you are able to truly recognize and respond to your feelings with wisdom, you make choices that align with your values and priorities for a more fulfilling life.

Improving how we understand feelings is a lifelong journey that needs patience, self-reflection, and an open mind to keep learning. Making this effort provides rich benefits in both our personal and professional lives. It also shapes us to become more thoughtful, caring, and well-rounded people.

Gaining deeper insight into emotions is hugely important for getting along better with others, making wise choices, and feeling fulfilled. Crucial skills include self-awareness, self-control, and empathy. These let us navigate relationships smoothly and find greater satisfaction.

One foundation is self-awareness—noticing your own feelings and what sparks them. This involves regularly checking in with yourself, whether through journaling, meditation, or just taking time to observe your thoughts and emotions. The more you understand your inner landscape, the better you can recognize triggers and handle yourself accordingly.

For example, you may get anxious before big meetings. Self-reflection helps you realize your anxiety often stems from fearing how others will see you. Knowing this gives you the power to prepare more, use stress-reducing strategies, or change your perspective to focus on value additions instead of failures.

Closely linked is self-regulation—guiding your emotions in a way aligned with goals. This might mean techniques for intense feelings, such as deep breaths before replying during conflicts. It also helps avoid regrets by recognizing and redirecting self-defeating patterns.

Imagine a colleague's comment offends you. Strong self-control allows you to hit pause, consider your reaction, and respond thoughtfully rather than impulsively lashing out. This keeps interactions constructive.

Continually refining skills like self-awareness and self-regulation empowers handling life's complexities with empathy, composure, and care for yourself and others along the journey.

Empathy is another crucial skill for understanding feelings. It allows for building stronger bonds through caring about others' experiences. Developing empathy takes work.

You must truly listen to people instead of waiting for your turn to reply. Pay attention to how they act as well as what they say. Try seeing situations from their perspective. This provides deeper insight into how they feel.

Imagine a teammate struggling with deadlines. Empathy means realizing their stress probably comes from too much work or personal issues outside their control instead of laziness. You can show understanding, lend support, and work together for solutions.

Active listening is a powerful way to boost emotional intelligence and comprehension. It involves focusing only on the speaker, asking clarifying questions, and repeating what you heard to confirm. Active listening shows you care about what they have to say and that they feel listened to and understood.

Making an effort to care about others' feelings fosters quality connections. When people sense they are seen and supported, interactions go smoother with less judgment and more care for one another. This requires daily effort to tune into those around you through your full presence and compassion.

Our words only tell part of the story; how someone's body looks and sounds provides important clues, too. Paying attention to nonverbal signals gives deeper insight beyond just what's said. Things like posture, facial expressions, and tone of voice unconsciously reveal feelings and thoughts.

Have you ever noticed someone with their shoulders hunched and their eyes down during a talk? That slumped pose may mean they feel uneasy or anxious. A friend with arms folded could be signaling discomfort in their environment. Raised eyebrows and pursed lips commonly show confusion over an issue.

Beyond single motions, watch how energy levels and physical engagement rise and fall. High energy, like rapid arm movements, indicates excitement, while slow, sluggish actions match dejection. Withdrawing into their shell or fidgeting frequently hints at inner tension.

Of course, tones paint a picture as vividly as postures. Happy conversations flow in upbeat melodies while stressful topics darken to grave notes. Accusations sharpen the voice just as questions lift it inquisitively. Calm reassurances soothe with soothing tempos.

Combine the physical cues with tone, and you will gain a rich emotional snapshot of the person. Are they leaning in with rapt focus and eager tones? Then they're invested in the exchange. But slumped back dismissively while the tone dragged—disinterest likely reigns.

Taking time to observe nonverbals brings conversations to a deeper human level of understanding one another. It allows us to see beneath surface words to appreciate another's true experience in the moment.

The more you notice these unconscious signs, the more attuned you become to subtle changes in color interactions. With practice, you'll pick up on frustrations earlier or comfort someone preemptively when you notice their mood darkening.

Overall, nonverbal listening promotes empathy. It helps you walk in another's shoes and sense how they genuinely feel instead of just what they say. This enriched perception means you can form emotionally intelligent responses that strengthen relationships through care, insight, and care.

Ultimately, the journey of improving our understanding of emotions and enhancing our emotional intelligence is an ongoing process that requires dedication, self-reflection, and a willingness to learn and grow. By developing these critical skills, we can build stronger, more fulfilling relationships, make more informed decisions, and cultivate a greater sense of personal and professional success.

Whether we're navigating the complexities of our personal lives or the challenges of the workplace, the ability to interpret emotions accurately and respond with empathy and emotional intelligence can be a powerful tool for personal and professional development. By embracing this journey, we can become more effective, compassionate, and well-rounded individuals, better equipped to navigate the ever-changing landscape of our lives.

CHAPTER 3

THE IMPORTANCE OF EMOTIONAL AWARENESS

"When dealing with people, remember you are not dealing with creatures of logic, but with creatures of emotions."

-Dale Carnegie

Our emotions are complex reactions that involve both physical sensations in our bodies and mental thoughts and feelings in our minds. Emotions can be positive feelings like joy, happiness, or excitement. They can also be negative feelings like anger, sadness, or fear. The first step to understanding our emotions better is simply recognizing the different emotions we experience. We have to put names to the feelings we have to really be aware of them.

Our emotions serve three main roles. One role is as a survival mechanism; emotions help us respond when we sense danger or opportunity. Feeling afraid alerts us to potential threats, so we can protect ourselves. Feeling drawn to something encourages us to pursue its benefits. The second role is communication; emotions signal how we feel internally to others. When we appear mad, others know to give us space. Smiling conveys friendliness. The third role is in decision-making; emotions guide our choices and judgments. We may avoid something that may bring up sad memories, even if it's logical. Feeling optimistic can help us take chances.

Developing self-awareness of our emotions takes some inner reflection. Self-reflection means looking inward at our own thoughts, feelings, and behaviors to better understand ourselves. Making self-reflection a regular habit helps us learn to recognize our emotional responses more easily over time. A few techniques that can aid self-reflection include journaling daily about our experiences and the emotions tied to them. Repeated feelings may become clear by writing down how we felt during certain events or interactions. Mindfulness meditation also helps with self-reflection by training us to observe our emotions non-judgmentally in the present moment rather than getting caught up in reactions.

Keeping a daily journal is one of the most effective self-reflection tools. Writing a short entry each night allows us to look back at the highs and lows of the day. Detailing how different situations made us feel physically in our bodies and mentally in our thoughts brings emotions out of our subconscious to consciously examine. Over time, patterns may emerge, showing what types of events routinely spark certain feelings. This increased awareness of our emotional triggers enables us to better understand the roots of our reactions.

Practicing mindfulness meditation builds on self-reflection skills. Setting aside even just 10–15 minutes a day to focus only on our breathing trains the wandering mind. When distracting thoughts or feelings arise, mindfulness teaches us to simply acknowledge them without getting caught up in storms. We passively observe the sensations and return focus to breathing. Gradually, this builds a capacity to watch emotions from a distance without instinctively reacting or attaching strong judgments. Like looking at passing clouds, feelings can be recognized clearly and accepted as temporary natural responses. Mindfulness cultivates a calm awareness of ourselves from within.

With regular journaling and meditation, self-reflection leads to seeing our internal emotional landscape more like observing weather patterns than being swept up in every storm. We gain insights into our hot buttons and how to cool heated reactions. Recognizing recurring feelings and their triggers empowers us to consciously adjust behaviors to improve well-being and relationships. Emotional awareness, supported through self-reflection, allows us to steer our ship gently rather than remain adrift on every wave of emotion that comes. Making time daily for tools like journaling and mindfulness meditation provides reservoirs to draw from in weathering life's complex storms with equanimity.

Recognizing our emotions is an important part of building self-awareness. However, many people struggle to accurately identify what they're feeling. Having an expanded emotional vocabulary can help with this. Using lists that describe a wide range of emotions can give us more precise labels for our feelings. Emotion wheels are also useful - these categorize emotions into primary and secondary groups to pinpoint our state. Going through the list and wheel exercises regularly practices our ability to name our internal experiences.

Our emotions often show up physically before we're consciously aware of them. Tuning into body sensations provides clues about how we truly feel. Doing a body scan during meditation teaches awareness of tension or discomfort, which may relate to underlying feelings. Keeping a physical sensations journal pairs notes on how our body feels with the linked emotions. Over time, we learn to "read" our body like a barometer of our inner world.

Exploring what triggers our reactions helps us manage them better. Maintaining a trigger log records events that stir strong feelings. Reflection on why certain people or situations impact us that way reveals deeper emotional patterns. Looking for themes across triggers provides an understanding of core concerns. With this insight, alternative coping strategies can be developed for the next time a trigger occurs.

Building empathy aids emotional competence. Empathy means connecting with others through respectfully understanding their experience. Active listening closely focuses on the speaker rather than just waiting to reply. Observing body language and reflecting on what might be felt internally helps "read between the lines." Considering a situation from others' perspectives also gives a fuller picture of their emotions. These skills strengthen relationships and help resolve conflicts compassionately.

Overall, self-reflection develops self-awareness over time through simple daily practices. Taking time to tune inward and interact contemplatively with others cultivates emotional intelligence foundations like identification, awareness, understanding triggers, and building empathy. While inner work feels unglamorous compared to distractions, its rewards include enhanced well-being, clearer thinking, and richer connections to the people in our lives.

While reflecting inwardly is important, putting emotional awareness into practice reinforces what we learn. Setting aside time each day for emotional journaling allows deeper exploration of our feelings. Writing about specific events, interactions, or daily experiences and describing the emotions felt in detail provides insights over time. Patterns may emerge, showing recurring themes in one's emotional world.

Mindfulness is another key practice. Slowing down with focused breathing or meditation increases present-moment awareness, including our internal state. Using guided meditations geared toward emotions offers a structured way to introspect. Brief "mindful moments" throughout the day to check in also aid understanding of constantly changing feelings.

Role-playing emotional scenarios with others gives a safe space to experiment with expressing and processing feelings. Partners or small groups can take turns drawing emotion cards and acting out how that state may appear. Gauging reactions from those observing provides an outside perspective, too. Afterward, discussing both roles grants a greater understanding of both expressing and perceiving emotions.

Being aware of oneself is enriched through sharing with empathetic others. Creating an "emotion circle" allows taking turns discussing noteworthy experiences from journal entries, meditations, or role plays while the group actively listens without judgment. Participants can offer thoughtful questions to draw out deeper meanings or affirmations of growth. Over multiple sessions, this cultivates a supportive community for ongoing personal and social development.

Practicing feeling identification and reflection builds vocabulary for subtle gradations between emotions, which aids clear communication. Discussing misunderstandings helps recognize where words alone lack nuance, while adding gestures, tone, or context fills gaps. Meanwhile, nonverbal mirroring during talk time reflects back the emotional essence, showing empathic engagement helps express understanding even without words.

Incorporating creativity further enriches emotional processing. Drawing, movement, music, and storytelling tap right brain capacities. Integrating these modalities allows emotions to surface and be soothed in their own language before translating internally. Journaling with photos, colors, or symbols representing inner experiences bypasses the limitations of only words. Art also creates souvenirs to appreciate progress over time.

Regular emotional check-ins, mindfulness, role plays, sharing circles, and creative outlets form a toolkit for self-knowledge. With a commitment to daily practice, awareness increases naturally over weeks through reflection, expression, discussion, and play. Our inherent wisdom blossoms as the mind and heart become steadily closer friends.

Another helpful practice is creating empathy maps for people in one's regular circles. Taking time to consider others' feelings, needs, and concerns from their perspective cultivates understanding beyond surface-level interactions. Building this capacity for perspective-taking strengthens relationships and reduces conflict.

Engaging in volunteer work involving direct contact with people experiencing diverse emotions also fosters empathy abilities. By assuming a helper role, one is exposed to a range of human experiences. This could involve assisting in areas like community centers, hospitals, or crisis hotlines. Interacting compassionately with others facing challenges promotes gratitude for one's own situation, while learning empathy is a shared condition.

Developing emotional awareness is an ongoing process that requires patience, regular practice, and dedication over time. While not a quick fix, incorporating strategies like journaling, meditation, self-reflection, role-playing, creative expression, and building empathy provides a solid foundation. With daily commitment, insights emerge naturally through expression, discussion, and play rather than force. Our emotional intelligence deepens as the mind and heart grow closer in friendship through the gentle nurturing of self-understanding.

As awareness is enhanced, so are skills for understanding and managing feelings, which lead to healthy, fulfilling relationships and a strong sense of self. Connecting with emotions provides insights, allowing one to respond constructively to life's difficulties rather than just reacting on impulse or habit. This supports well-being, clarity of thought, and richness in relationships with oneself and others. While development never ends, the steady application of various awareness practices over weeks and months cultivates a natural bloom of one's inherent emotional wisdom.

CHAPTER 4

RECOGNIZING AND MANAGING YOUR EMOTIONS

"Some of the greatest moments in human history were fueled by emotional intelligence."

-Adam Grant

Understanding our emotions is so important for living a happy, healthy life. When I first started learning about this, it opened my eyes to how I'd been ignoring what was happening inside me for so long. I thought feeling sad or angry was something to push down, but I realized these emotions try to tell us something if we listen.

It begins with paying more attention to what you feel in different situations. Sometimes it's obvious, like being excited about a fun upcoming event. But other times it's more subtle, like feeling uneasy when talking to your boss even though nothing bad happened. Naming feelings with precise words like worried or anxious instead of just saying "not good" makes them clearer.

Another big breakthrough for you is separating out thoughts from feelings. Tell yourself, "I'm stupid for feeling this way," when really that's just a thought, not the feeling itself. Allowing yourself to feel sad or mad without immediately judging it as wrong can be freeing. Now, you can identify the emotion and then decide how to respond to it rationally rather than letting it control you.

Managing emotions is a lifelong skill, but meditation can be very helpful. Even five minutes of breathing and letting thoughts come and go have calmed you down when you're super riled up. Going for a walk, calling a friend, or writing in a journal also helps you process what you're experiencing, so strong feelings don't overwhelm you.

Sometimes, what we're upset about isn't even the real issue. For example, if you're stressed about work, it could be because you need more downtime for yourself than you might be making space for. Problem-solving the root cause puts you in the driver's seat instead of feelings dictating your actions. Approaching problems and setbacks optimistically as a challenge to overcome builds your confidence to handle whatever comes next.

Being your own cheerleader through hard times with self-compassion has changed everything. You no longer beat yourself up over emotional mistakes but gently guide yourself to a better headspace. Surrounding yourself with good people who have your back lifts you up, too. While learning will always be ongoing, making emotional intelligence a daily focus brings more peace. I'm grateful to finally understand this side of life I have been neglecting for so long.

Recognize the Inner Voice

Being able to identify and communicate our emotions is so important. Too often, people just say things like "I'm feeling good" or "I'm not feeling great." But these vague descriptions don't really convey much. It's like those memes telling dad jokes—you know the punchline won't have much depth!

When we limit our emotional vocabulary, it makes it harder for us to understand ourselves and for others to understand us. Think about how much clearer a conversation could be if you said, "I'm upset" instead of "I'm feeling frustrated right now." Or rather, "I'm happy," sharing that you feel excited or delighted at that moment.

Using more precise emotional words is kind of like upgrading your smartphone—you go from the basic functions to much richer features. It gives you a whole new level of awareness about what's really going on underneath the surface. No longer are feelings just simplistic categories of good versus bad.

I work with kids and see how limiting their emotional language impacts them. If a kid is just called "sad" all the time, they don't learn all the nuances, such as how feeling disappointed is different from feeling mournful.

As adults, we can also gain perspective on ourselves by expanding how we describe what's happening internally. Feeling blue versus feeling down in the dumps conveys different intensities. Being anxious versus nervous captures unique qualities in our mindset. The most obvious one is how distinguishing between being irritated and angry can change conflict outcomes for the better!

When you put more precision into your emotional terms, it just facilitates discussions so much. Rather than people thinking, "Oh, they're happy, so there's no problem," you can recognize that joy could have anxious elements too worthy of discussion. It stops assumptions and encourages truly understanding each other at a deeper level.

While increasing your emotional vocabulary takes effort, the rewards are immense. It puts you in the driver's seat of recognizing your internal experiences accurately so you can address them effectively.

We all know that feeling when our emotions start to get the better of us. Your heart rate rises, your thoughts race, and you just want to act immediately without thinking. Whether it's anger, sadness, or frustration, strong feelings can really take over in the heat of the moment.

But did you know that just pausing for a brief time is one of the most effective things you can do to regain control? Even waiting a mere 60 seconds before responding or reacting can make a world of difference in how you handle things. In those precious moments, your prefrontal cortex has time to re-engage, so you don't just instinctively react.

Think about the last time road rage nearly took over when someone cut you off. Or how ready you were to fire back at that insensitive comment from a family member? If only, in those intense situations, you hit the emotional brakes for a bit before accelerating your behavior. With pause, you allow yourself to take a step back and look at what's truly going on from a less reactive place.

I know that for me, the pause has been a total game-changer. I used to let my anxiety or insecurity run wild with no filter. But these days, as soon as my body starts flipping that "fight or flight" switch, I deliberately calm my breathing and give myself space. It isn't always easy when adrenaline is pumping, but I've come to recognize my trigger signs that it's time to step away and gain clarity.

You might go for a quick walk, do some chores, or call a supportive friend—whatever you need to remove yourself from the heightened intensity, even briefly. The goal is to diffuse just enough to access your wiser, more considerate thinking and prevent words or actions you'll later regret. I promise the pause will pay off in avoiding unnecessary escalation or damage to relationships time and again.

As with any new skill, consciously implementing emotional pause takes practice. However, over time, it can become second nature to create that natural divide between feeling and acting. You train yourself to respond thoughtfully rather than just reacting impulsively in the heat of strong emotions. So next time you feel yourself starting to see red, I encourage you to breathe deeply and tap the brakes before moving forward again in a healthy way. A brief pause just might be your best tool for gaining back control.

Deep Breathing and Switching the Pattern

Deep breathing is seriously underrated in its power to relieve stress and tension in the body. Taking slow, deep breaths all the way down to your belly for 5 minutes quiets your nervous system and lowers your fight or flight response. I like to pair it with muscle relaxation—consciously relaxing one muscle group from my toes up at a time. Visualization can also transport you to somewhere peaceful as you breathe, like a calm beach or forest. Whatever method works, focus on releasing physical tension you may not even realize you're holding.

Shifting negative thought patterns is another game-changer. When something happens, and you automatically think, "This is awful, " pause and see if you can reframe the situation more positively. If that scary presentation makes you super nervous, see it as a way to help people rather than something you'll fail at. Changing your mindset, even in small ways, alters your emotional reaction. Perspective is so powerful.

Healthy Habits Ensures a Healthy Life

It's also vital to have healthy outlets to process feelings, whether through exercise, creative hobbies, spiritual practices, or talking to understanding people. Go for a run to burn off frustration, immerse yourself in a craft to lift sadness, or call a good friend to vent and get perspective. Make sure to do things you genuinely find meaningful and fulfilling rather than numbing distractions. Finding passion-based ways to channel your inner experience outward leads to so much growth.

You take charge of your emotional well-being by using various techniques to relax the body and shift thinking, then express yourself creatively through interests and social support. Aim to make them habits, so you have go-to methods during challenging times. With practice, you'll be better able to handle whatever feelings come your way.

Problem-Solving Methods

"If you change the way you look at things, the things you look at change."

– Dr. Wayne Dyer

Whenever negative emotions start to take over, it's always a good idea to try and get to the root of what's really causing them. You might be stressed because of conflicts at work that need resolution or maybe sad because of a lack of social connection you can address. Figuring out the underlying issues is the first step to feeling more in control.

From there, brainstorm practical solutions rather than just hoping the feelings will pass on their own. If a particular task keeps causing anxiety, see if you can delegate or modify it to make it feel less overwhelming. If family dynamics leave you feeling down, have caring conversations to establish better boundaries. Getting to the root and problem-solving empowers you to make positive adjustments that lift your mood.

Of course, while tackling triggering situations, be sure to also show yourself compassion. It's all too easy to add pressure or put yourself down for normal human emotions in hard times. But feeling sad, angry, or stressed does not define your worth. Your feelings are valid, and you deserve kindness, even from your own self-talk.

Make a conscious effort to use gentle, supportive language when you're struggling inside. "It's okay to feel this way. I'm taking good care of myself right now." If you slip up, praise your efforts to improve difficult areas rather than harsh critiques. Being your best friend through ups and downs goes a long way.

Nurturing calmness and caring for yourself gives your mind and body much-needed relief from distress. Make soothing rituals like cozy baths, meditation, or relaxing with special people or activities a priority on hard days. Expressing gratitude for small joys also lifts your perspective. Self-care sends the reassuring message that you're not alone in your inner experience.

With problem-solving, self-care, and acceptance, you build a strong support system for your emotional well-being, even during lonely moments. Over time, negative feelings lose their power while your resilience grows. So focus on identifying what you need, addressing root issues, and speaking to yourself with empathy and care. Your heart and mental health will thank you.

Emotional resilience is adapting well to stress and challenges while staying emotionally healthy. Building resilience involves nurturing relationships that provide emotional support and having close friends, family, and colleagues. I also maintain a hopeful outlook by focusing on my strengths and being grateful and peaceful even during difficulties. Establishing good boundaries protects energy by saying no to draining people or activities and making time for relaxing pursuits. Seeing change as natural and a chance to learn and grow allows us to fully benefit from emotional intelligence.

Something I've found really helpful in maintaining emotional health is scheduling regular time for self-reflection and check-ins. Whether it's journaling each night or having weekly "me" sessions, consciously focusing on my internal experiences keeps me accountable.

It helps me identify patterns—did certain situations consistently cause stronger reactions this week? Are there emotions I tend to ignore or push down that need extra attention and care? Reflection illuminates areas for growth so I can build the skills I need most.

Daily check-ins where I rate my stress and mood levels on a scale are also insightful. On busy weeks, I notice dips that signal when to slow down or try relaxing techniques. Or a few green days in a row reinforce what's been going well for me. Plus, it's rewarding to look back monthly and see tangible progress!

Sharing how I genuinely feel with caring people and actively listening to them does wonders, too. Instead of hiding behind bravado or complaining, letting others bear witness to my full range of emotions in a supportive space fills my cup back up. The same goes for keeping communication lines open when something upsets me; respectfully working through issues prevents resentment.

Continuous education and enrichment are equally critical for long-term wellness. Whether reading about new coping strategies, attending therapy workshops, or seeking counseling during major life changes, I commit to lifelong learning to understand myself and others better. Evolving is how we grow our capacity for healthy relationships, resilience, and joy.

Overall, integrating daily mindfulness, self-reflection, and meaningful exchange helps me apply emotional skills optimally. Maintaining this focus allows skills to become second nature, so I can handle whatever comes my way. My commitment is to this ongoing growth work.

While it's a lifelong journey of growth, making conscious efforts like expanding your vocabulary, reflecting regularly, and addressing issues rather than pushing them down will serve you tremendously well in relationships, career, and overall well-being.

Developing awareness of your internal experiences is truly empowering. Instead of letting outside forces dictate your moods, you gain understanding and authority over how you move through this world. Committing to incorporating relaxation, communication, problem-solving, and compassion when difficulties arise will strengthen your resilience over time.

Be patient and gentle with yourself as these techniques become habits. Nobody has emotions 100% figured out - we're all growing each day. But simply making the exploration of your inner life a priority sets you ahead of the curve. Remembering that you're not alone in these experiences and that we all have moments of imperfection may offer comfort when perfectionism creeps in.

While emotional skills are deeply personal, connecting with others on a journey of understanding ourselves and each other holds incredible potential for positive change, too. Imagine communities where vulnerability and honesty about our feelings were encouraged over stoicism and "toughing it out." Imagine the relief and healing relationships that could emerge if emotions like frustration or fear were deemed valuable signals to address rather than suppress.

CHAPTER 5

DEVELOPING EMPATHY

"Whenever you feel like criticizing any one...just remember that all the people in this world haven't had the advantages that you've had."

— F. Scott Fitzgerald

Understanding how others feel is key to forming meaningful connections. While showing care and concern for someone in distress is kind, truly understanding their perspective can make a bigger difference. There is a distinction between sympathizing with someone and truly feeling what they feel. Sympathy involves recognizing another person's emotions, like sadness or pain, from an outside perspective. In contrast, empathy means imagining their internal experience, picturing their thoughts and emotions as if they were your own.

Empathy requires more than acknowledging someone's feelings; it involves stepping into their shoes to understand how their experiences shape their current views and challenges. This ability takes practice, as we naturally see the world from our own perspective. It challenges us to consider realities beyond our own.

However, empathy does not mean taking on another's burdens or losing yourself in their troubles. Instead, it's about understanding their point of view to offer meaningful, tailored support. Empathizing involves stepping back from assumptions and preconceptions to truly gain insight into another's experience. While sympathy is an external expression of feeling, empathy is an active connection with someone's experience on a deeper level.

To enhance empathy, start by building self-awareness. Recognize traits like optimism, patience, or sensitivity in yourself and consider how these may differ from others' perspectives. Acknowledging our limits helps us approach others more respectfully and seek more information without judgment. Making assumptions can undermine empathy; listening without judgment helps to gain a clearer understanding.

Practicing empathy in daily interactions strengthens our ability to connect. Observing body language, facial expressions, and tone of voice reveals emotions beyond words. Being attentive to how you affect others shows care for their comfort. Considering why beliefs or opinions exist allows for deeper understanding beyond initial impressions. Assuming good intent maintains an open-minded approach.

Like building any skill, developing empathy takes regular practice. Small, consistent efforts are more effective than occasional large attempts. Over time, perspective-taking becomes instinctual, forming relationships based on mutual understanding rather than misunderstandings. By walking in another's shoes, empathy fosters compassion, benefiting both the giver and the receiver.

Understanding the Components of Empathy

While empathy can seem like a single concept, it's actually made up of different parts. Fully understanding someone's perspective involves three main elements: cognitive, emotional, and compassionate empathy. Each plays an important role in connecting with others on a deeper level.

Cognitive empathy is using your brainpower to see a situation from another person's viewpoint. It involves imagining their situation and trying to understand their thinking, even if you can't relate to their experiences. The focus is on comprehending cognitively rather than sharing their emotions. Developing cognitive skills like listening without bias and questioning preconceived notions strengthens this ability to "stand in someone else's shoes."

Emotional empathy takes it a step further by feeling what someone else feels. When you can emotionally echo and share in their reactions, you experience true attunement. This bond taps hidden wells of compassion that motivate meaningful support. Of course, taking on another's full emotional burden risks losing your own boundaries. Healthy expression involves perceiving emotional undertones accurately rather than becoming overwhelmed yourself.

Compassionate empathy activates the deepest caring response. It couples a genuine understanding of how experiences uniquely shape each journey with heartfelt empathy for life's shared struggles. Where cognitive empathy focuses on perspective and emotional empathy taps feelings, compassionate empathy is motivated by action. Beyond recognizing suffering, it's the driving force behind alleviating pain through kindness, respect, forgiveness, and grace wherever possible.

While these three components support each other, it's also important to recognize each on its own. For example, grasping someone's situation intellectually without syncing emotions or connecting compassionately is possible. Someone who articulates could dissect viewpoints without true attunement. And empathy isn't the same as forgiveness—one can understand without pardoning. When developed together in balance, cognitive, emotional, and compassionate empathy are powerful.

Practicing each type strengthens skills like active listening, suspending judgments, and recognizing nuance. Cognitive training helps bypass surface assessments. Regular exposure to new ideas stretches old boundaries. Emotional practice tunes our interpretations of body language, tone, and subtext. Recognizing our instincts keeps reason foremost. Expressing care compassionately without projections or expectations transforms understanding into humanity.

How Empathy Heals Broken Bonds

You know, being able to understand what someone else is going through is so valuable in so many ways. When you can empathize with people, your relationships all around are better. Communicating and connecting on a deeper level is what empathy is all about.

And relationships are really everything, aren't they? Whether it's family, friends, or coworkers, we all need those bonds to feel happy and supported. However, relationships take work, and empathy is like the glue that holds them together. Trying to see things from another person's perspective shows you care about how they see things, too. That kind of understanding and respect build a lot of trust.

Empathy also improves how we work through problems and conflicts with others. Instead of just standing your ground, you consider where the other side is coming from before deciding what to do. That makes it way more likely that you can find a good solution and feel good about it. It prevents a lot of unnecessary arguing and hurt feelings.

Our mental and emotional well-being benefits a lot from being empathetic, too. It's healthy for us to think beyond our own experience now and then. Plus, focusing on other people's lives helps keep our own issues in perspective. That sort of perspective reduces stress and makes us feel happier overall.

And have you noticed how empathy seems to inspire more helpful behaviors? When we take the time to feel what someone else might be going through, we're more motivated to lend a hand if they need one. Empathy cultivates compassion—that natural desire to alleviate suffering in others. And communities where people look out for each other and help their neighbors are just better places to live overall.

So, whether it's personal relationships, resolving conflicts, mental health, or even encouraging good deeds, empathy pays off. And really, what does it cost to try to understand where someone else is coming from before jumping to conclusions? A little effort can go a long way. We can all work on empathy, and every little bit makes a difference in our interactions with others.

The more you practice empathy, the more it becomes your natural way of relating to people. Spreading more empathy around the world seems like a good way to make our little part of it a kinder place overall. So keep broadening your perspective, my friends; our communities are surely better for every act of understanding between us.

Moving on, understanding empathy on a deeper level is really interesting when you look at what's actually going on in our brains and bodies. Science has recently learned a lot about how our minds work to let us connect with each other. For example, did you know there are special neurons called "mirror neurons" that play a big role?

Mirror neurons are cells in our frontal and parietal lobes that activate when we do something, like lift a hand, and when we see someone else doing it, too! Just watching someone's expression or movement seems to trigger our own brain and body to "mirror" or simulate what that other person is experiencing. It's pretty cool how we're wired to instinctively feel similar sensations just by observing someone else.

Scientists think these mirror neurons may help explain how infants learn so quickly from imitating adults. They also help our brains internally "practice" reading emotions and interpreting social cues to better recognize feelings in others that we're familiar with in ourselves. Simply paying attention and watching what people do seems to give our brains the practice of feeling similar states.

Some research even shows that our autonomic nervous system can become empathetic. Things like pupillary responses, heart rate, breathing, and perspiration have been observed to change slightly but noticeably when we focus intently on someone else's emotional experience. It's like our bodies automatically start to share and feel with the other person on a basic physical level through these mirroring systems.

The more we study mirror neurons, the more it seems they play a big role, allowing us to instantly "feel with" other minds. They give us that natural ability to sense what might be going on internally for someone just from their outside presentation. Some scientists believe impairment in mirroring abilities could contribute to reduced empathy, which is seen in some disorders, too.

It's so cool to think our natural empathy and social skills emerge so fundamentally from how our mirror neurons, brain, and body all link up to represent others' experiences within ourselves. It is fascinating to see what science reveals about how deeply intuitive and reflexive compassion can be for humans when our default biological settings aren't disrupted. Nature certainly designed us to look out for each other!

Understanding these behind-the-scenes mechanisms helps us appreciate empathy's importance even more. While we can consciously work to broaden our perspectives, too, so much of our capacity to connect with others relies on inherent traits we may not fully realize.

The Theory of Mind

Developing empathy involves some pretty neat mental skills. One amazing thing we can do is understand that other people have different thoughts and feelings than we do—it's called the "theory of mind." From a young age, we realize that not everyone sees or knows what we see and know.

Having a theory of mind means you get that just because you feel excited about something doesn't mean your friend feels the same way. Or just because you think one answer on a test is right doesn't mean the teacher thinks that. It's wild that we eventually figured out there are other minds with totally separate ideas!

And being able to see things from someone else's perspective gets even trickier when you throw emotions into the mix. Our feelings aren't always rational, you know? That's where emotional contagion comes in. Basically, emotions have a way of spreading between people, like, well, contagions.

A lot of times, we can literally "catch" feelings from others without even realizing it. Have you ever noticed that being around really happy people tends to put you in a good mood, too? Or how can sadness, stress, or anger sometimes seem to rub off? Scientists have proven emotions can be infectious between humans through facial expressions, tones of voice, body language, and more.

It's pretty cool, but it is also important to realize how much emotional contagion influences us. If we're not careful, we can find ourselves taking on stronger feelings than the situation calls for, mirroring someone else's state. However, being aware of contagion also lets us appreciate how little acts of kindness, humor, or compassion go a long way in lifting each other up.

Developing Empathy

There are several approaches someone can take to strengthen their ability to understand others' perspectives and experiences.

Active listening is key—fully focusing on what the other person is saying without distraction and providing feedback to show you're engaged. Asking open-ended questions can provide useful context.

Perspective-taking enhances the dilemma; truly imagining "walking in someone else's shoes" by considering the unique factors that have shaped their life journey is also important.

Beyond words, paying attention to body language, tone of voice, and other nonverbal cues gives additional insight into what someone may be feeling but is not saying directly.

Taking time each day to slow down and be present, whether through meditation, yoga, or other mindful practices, helps cultivate awareness of inner thoughts and outer stimuli. This increased awareness allows for more thoughtful responses instead of knee-jerk reactions when dealing with difficult situations. Reading widely, especially works of fiction where readers take on the roles of different characters, strengthens our ability to connect with those unlike ourselves. No one can claim to understand another's feelings perfectly, but making an effort through reflective listening builds mutual understanding over time.

Small acts of kindness, without expectation of something in return, help foster caring about others' well-being. Holding doors, offering a smile or words of encouragement, volunteering or donating to help those in need—these everyday gestures reinforce our shared humanity. Reflecting regularly on positive and negative interactions highlights opportunities for growth. With patience and consistency, skills like considering multiple viewpoints, regulating emotional responses, and forming meaningful connections can be strengthened. While there's always room for improvement, focusing on others with empathy, respect, and good faith goes a long way.

Overcoming Barriers

While developing empathy has many benefits, it's important to acknowledge that it doesn't come easily for everyone. Our minds have a tendency to automatically make quick judgments and generalizations about people based on surface-level details. These cognitive biases can seriously impair our ability to walk in another's shoes if we're not aware of them.

One extremely common bias is in-group favoritism, the natural inclination to view your own social groups more positively than others. This causes us to relate more easily to those who are similar to us. Another is confirmation bias, where we pay more attention to information that aligns with our existing beliefs and dismiss anything contradictory. When interacting with someone with an opposing view, it's too easy to discount their perspective entirely.

Then there's stereotyping—making broad generalizations about large groups without considering individual differences. We've all been guilty of thinking, "All people from X place must be like Y" at some point. While stereotypes may sometimes seem harmless on the surface, they prevent true understanding of others as complex human beings. If you find yourself doing these things, don't be too hard on yourself; recognizing our biases is the first step. From there, challenge preconceived notions by actively seeking out new information.

Another hurdle is simply becoming overwhelmed by strong emotions coming from one another. Sometimes, listening to someone else's distressing experiences can stir up our own difficult feelings. Other times, intense displays of anger or sadness are just uncomfortable to engage with directly. The key is establishing healthy personal boundaries while still being empathetic. You don't need to take on others' burdens to express care and support. It's okay to step away briefly if you need to process your reaction before responding constructively.

Lack of exposure to diversity is another empathy roadblock for some. Interacting mainly with those identical to you provides limited practice considering alternate mindsets. While immersing yourself in other communities may not always be feasible, small steps like supporting inclusive events, traveling locally, and broadening your media diet can help. Even online, seeking out respectful discussions across lines of difference nourishes empathy muscles.

The beauty of empathy is that, with effort, we can all work to overcome our innate biases and limitations. No one expects you to understand another's life fully on the first try. But with patience, humility, and determination—attributes empathy itself promotes—barriers gradually start falling away. Extending good faith to understand one another is key to building the compassionate, interconnected society we all wish to see.

We've covered a lot in our discussion about what empathy means, why it's important, common misunderstandings, existing barriers, and practical steps anyone can take to strengthen this essential skill. No matter where you're starting from on this journey, this book will transform your lens to see empathy not as something abstract but as a very real tool for building greater emotional intelligence and improving your relationships.

While developing true empathy is an ongoing process that takes commitment, focusing your efforts with intention and purpose can yield meaningful results much sooner than you think. Be patient with yourself as you challenge past mindsets and step out of your comfort zone. Small acts of opening your mind each day are what build real growth over time. Remember that no one is perfect, and we all have room for improvement. Approach this endeavor with compassion for where you and others currently are.

As with any new skill, cultivate regular opportunities to practice and reinforce your learning about empathy. Choose relationship environments where you can experiment with active listening, perspective-taking, inclusive language, and self-reflection without fear of judgment. Seek diversity of thought within safe communities dedicated to understanding different lived realities. Keep notes on misunderstandings that arise so you can revisit your assumptions and do better next time.

Let your empathy transform how you interact with close friends and family and those you may disagree with or see as "other." Approaching others on their terms instead of your own nourishes compassion. Extend empathy freely without expecting anything in return as a way to honor each person's humanity, regardless of surface traits. View interactions as chances to understand rather than be understood.

Throughout your journey, maintain empathy, not just for others but also for yourself. Own your shortcomings openly while focusing on consistent progress each day. Let your capacity for care, patience, and good faith stretch to include your whole self as well. In this way, personal and social growth become mutually reinforcing as your emotional intelligence blossoms.

With a dedication to sincere practice, empathy will start coming more naturally in even difficult situations over time. Its ripple effects, like enhanced communication, stronger bonds, and a knack for creative problem-solving, will benefit you and your relationships endlessly. Continue nurturing empathy within and allowing it to guide your interactions outward. Its gifts have only begun to emerge—how empowering to actively cultivate such a skill! I wish you the very best on your journey ahead.

CHAPTER 6

EMOTIONAL REGULATION TECHNIQUES

"Those (thoughts) that will not hear must be made to feel."
—German proverb

The ability to understand and process emotions is an important part of who we are as people. However, it's not just about knowing what we and others are feeling; we must also be able to control and react to those emotions in helpful, healthy ways. Managing our feelings so they enhance our lives rather than hinder us is called emotional regulation. Gaining skills in this area can serve us well in many situations.

When emotions flare up, it can be all too easy to act rashly or say things we later regret. However, learning techniques to regulate our feelings gives us power over them, rather than being powerless in their grip. If we want to make good decisions, stay calm in tough times, and maintain strong relationships, cultivating emotional regulation is key. There are several different methods one can practice to improve this important skill.

One approach is to take slow, deep breaths when feeling very excited or upset. Our breath is closely tied to our physical and mental state, so consciously controlling it with deep inhales and exhales can help lower our heart rate and relax tense muscles when stressed. Counting to 10 before responding to something upsetting is another simple yet effective tactic. The brief pause gives us space to think clearly rather than just reacting in the heat of the moment without considering the consequences.

Reflecting on what exactly triggered an emotional reaction can also be insightful. Was it really the event itself, or is something else bothering us below the surface? Understanding the root cause rather than just the symptoms helps address problems at their source. Talking through stressful situations with a trusted friend is another way to gain perspective, feel heard, and release built-up tension. Just verbalizing difficult feelings and events can be remarkably cathartic.

Making an effort to catch and reframe negative thought patterns is another technique. If we tend to catastrophize or believe the worst, we can mentally counter those thoughts by envisioning more balanced possibilities. Reminding ourselves of past challenges we overcame can instill confidence for facing present hurdles. Also, replacing harsh self-criticism with compassionate encouragement supports healthier emotional well-being. Approaching difficulties with patience, care for yourself, and optimism helps maintain a regulated mind.

While strong feelings are natural and unavoidable, we don't need to be at their mercy if we commit to developing emotional self-awareness and control skills. Regular practice of methods like deep breathing, reframing, and talking through issues with empathetic listeners are ways to gain dominance over intense emotions rather than letting them dominate us. An ability to consciously manage and direct our feelings serves us far better than being tossed helplessly by their unpredictable tides. Overall well-being, clear thinking, and healthy relationships depend on mastering this important life skill.

The Importance of Emotional Regulation in Daily Life

Managing our emotions isn't just about avoiding occasional meltdowns; it's a key part of everyday functioning and well-being. When we consider how much our moods and reactions impact simple daily interactions, it becomes clear why developing stronger emotional regulation is worth focusing on. Our emotions color nearly every experience, for better or worse, depending on how well we can guide them.

Just think about common activities like running errands, being with family, or going to work/school each day. Small annoyances are unavoidable, like traffic jams, long lines, or disagreements with others. But how we choose to respond internally makes all the difference. Someone with poor emotional control might broodingly stew over minor issues, let their frustration boil over, or engage in risky behaviors like road rage. However, with practice regulating feelings, we can acknowledge bothersome things calmly without being thrown off for hours.

Strong emotional regulation even impacts physical health. Unmanaged stress puts long-term wear and tear on our bodies through the constant activation of stress responses. But if we can diffuse tension through relaxation techniques when emotions start to escalate, it eases that burden. Mental wellness also benefits since stable moods are better for avoiding excessive worrying, self-criticism, or dependency on unhealthy coping mechanisms like substance use.

Relationships require emotional regulation, too. No one is perfect, and loved ones will inevitably annoy us at times through no real fault of their own. But reacting harshly or holding grudges over small transgressions strains close bonds. On the other hand, addressing issues respectfully after taking time to cool off can strengthen understanding between people who care about each other. Communication at work also flows more smoothly when colleagues remain composed during disagreements rather than personalizing every conflict.

None of us are robots; feelings are a natural byproduct of being human. However, cultivating awareness of our internal states and consciously adopting strategies to stabilize strong moods means we aren't totally at their mercy from moment to moment. Emotional regulation gives us breathing room to thoughtfully evaluate situations rather than just reflexively reacting. While completely eliminating all negative emotions may not be realistic or even ideal, improved self-management can still meaningfully influence daily experiences for the better. Even small wins like curbing annoyance from minor annoyances save us stress that accumulates over time. Mastering this important life skill truly pays dividends.

Emotional Regulation Techniques

Now that we understand how impactful emotional regulation can be in our daily lives, exploring specific methods one can employ to strengthen this ability is valuable. No single approach works best for everyone, and what helps may depend on an individual's temperament as well as the situation. Keeping a few different strategies in our toolbox allows us the flexibility to choose what fits a given scenario best. Regularly practicing these techniques also improves our proficiency over time, as emotional regulation, like any skill, requires consistent exercise.

Deep Breathing

Deep breathing is one of the most basic yet powerful techniques. When we start feeling stressed, worried, or upset, consciously slowing our respiration calms both body and mind. Inhaling deeply through the nose to a count of five, holding for a few seconds, then fully exhaling through pursed lips for five counts, quiets overactive thinking and reduces physiological signs of anxiety like increased heart rate. Repeating this pattern several times helps diffuse tension.

Soothing Visualization

Visualization can also shift heavy moods. Conjuring soothing mental images, whether real or imagined, transports us out of a distressing present. Picture relaxing settings like beaches, forests, or anything personally comforting. This redirects focus away from stressors. Similarly, self-talk modifies troubling thought patterns that fuel emotions. When negative scripts arise, we can consciously reframe them in a balanced, supportive way, similar to what we'd say encouragingly to a friend.

Speaking Out

Talking through problems verbalizes festering feelings to release built-up steam, gain an outside perspective on objective facts rather than our subjective experience, and feel less alone in difficult situations. A compassionate listener helps reframe issues in a more constructive light. Journaling provides a similar catharsis of putting worries down on paper away in private. Later, looking back brings insights on patterns to target for improved coping.

Engaging Activities

Staying active relieves tension stored physically in muscles better than rumination. Simple movement, whether cleaning, short walks outside, or yoga stretches, redistributes energy in a healthier direction than dwelling. Creative outlets funnel feelings productively through artistic, musical, or hands-on hobbies. Finding what we find personally meaningful can help us regain inner calm and perspective.

Gaining mastery over feelings enhances so many areas of our lives. As we've discussed, emotional regulation is important for everything from maintaining physical health and mental wellness to navigating relationships and daily responsibilities. While challenges will always exist and strong reactions may occasionally arise, developing a toolbox of strategies gives us power over how long we allow difficulties to derail us. Making a consistent effort to try techniques like deep breathing, self-talk, journaling, exercise, and other outlets shown through research to diffuse tension means we spend less time tossed helplessly by surfacing emotions. Over time, these practiced habits remand control from a primal reactionary mind to a wise, composed self. With emotional regulation, we no longer need to be defined by temporary feelings but can thoughtfully choose our responses instead. Life satisfaction, productivity, and longevity increase when we gain this important skill. While the journey requires commitment, each small success moves us closer to a calmer life lived deliberately rather than haphazardly at emotions' whims.

CHAPTER 7

BUILDING SELF-CONFIDENCE

"Start where you are. Use what you have. Do what you can."

—Arthur Ashe

Self-confidence is something we all strive for in life. It's that inner feeling that you can achieve your goals and handle whatever challenges come your way. Having confidence in yourself lays the foundation for other important skills, like emotional intelligence. When you believe in your abilities, it allows you to interact with others positively and better understand your emotions.

Developing self-confidence is important because it leads to greater happiness, less stress, and more fulfilling relationships. However, true confidence doesn't come from arrogance or pretending to be something you're not. It grows from an honest look at your strengths and weaknesses as well as acceptance of things outside your control. Staying grounded in reality while focusing on personal growth is key.

Some people think you're born with confidence, but that's not entirely true. It can be nurtured over time through small successes and experiences reinforcing your capabilities. Start by reflecting on past achievements, big or small, that show you already have skills to feel proud of. Remember that challenges are normal for everyone, and failure doesn't define you. Try keeping a journal of accomplishments to look back on when doubt creeps in.

Believing in yourself also means trusting your own judgment. Take time each day to assess how you handled different situations without being too critical. Noticing even gradual progress in tackling problems independently can boost assurance. Having an internal sense of control over your decisions and circumstances provides reassurance during change or uncertainty.

Another factor that boosts confidence is staying optimistic about how you frame future possibilities. Avoid negatively ruminating over "what ifs" and focus instead on your power to influence outcomes through effort and smart choices. Visualizing the achievement of goals step-by-step makes larger goals feel attainable. Remember that setbacks are inevitable, so just provide valuable feedback to redirect focus, not signs you've failed overall.

Of course, no one is perfect all the time. Even those with strong self-assurance have weaknesses to acknowledge and improve on. The key is not denying flaws but continuously working to manage areas that trip you up without harsh criticism. Accepting imperfection allows room for growth, while confidence encourages persistence through obstacles instead of avoidance. Striving for realistic assessments of liability neither overestimates nor underestimates what's reasonable to expect of yourself.

To truly benefit from self-confidence, it also involves accurately presenting it to others through how you carry yourself. Stand tall with an open, attentive posture, and interact with a pleasant tone that conveys being at ease. Smile sincerely, make eye contact in conversation, and think before speaking to show respect and confidence in what you have to say. Let your words match your actions by following through on the commitments you make. Over time, subtle adjustments to portray faith in yourself authentically end up positively influencing how people perceive and respond to you.

In closing, cultivating self-confidence is a lifelong pursuit but well worth it. Approaching each new challenge or relationship from a secure place of self-belief opens doors to fulfillment. Having confidence means embracing both strengths and imperfections to continuously develop into your best self. With a balanced view and working to nurture it from the inside out, true confidence cannot help but radiate and attract similar qualities in others.

While developing a strong sense of self-belief provides many advantages, having too little or too much confidence can also pose issues. Finding the right balance is important for well-being and relationships. Some struggle with constantly doubting themselves due to past failures or comparisons to others perceived as "better." This type of low self-confidence can hold people back from trying new activities and taking appropriate risks. It also affects how assertive one is when advocating for needs or facing unfair treatment.

Prolonged low confidence often stems from internalizing a harsh, critical inner voice that blows mistakes out of proportion. Negative self-talk breeds anxiety over making decisions or putting ideas forward for fear of judgment. While concerns are normal, an exaggerated worry that anything less than perfection will lead to disapproval can paralyze productivity. It helps in these situations to recognize negative thoughts as not facts and replace them consciously with evidence of competencies. Appreciating effort and growth as valuable in their own right lifts burdens to "always get it right."

At the opposite end lies overconfidence, which masquerades as assurance but risks alienating others. A swagger of never doubting one's opinions or needing assistance despite clear limitations breeds arrogance over time. While self-belief encourages action, exaggerated overconfidence cripples the ability to admit flaws, learn from errors, or value input beyond the individual perspective. It distances people who grow tired of the implications of their advice being unneeded or their perspectives invalid. Overconfidence spawns unnecessary power struggles instead of cooperation through mutual understanding.

The optimum level acknowledges capabilities realistically while leaving room for progress. It recognizes not having full mastery in every situation and seeks to supplement strengths with other talents. Flexible confidence can revise perceptions open-mindedly based on facts instead of dismissing anything that threatens their sense of self-worth. It conveys faith in continuing development versus resting on past successes, keeping perspectives fresh, and making relationships collaborative.

Maintaining equilibrium requires ongoing self-reflection about tendencies to overvalue or undervalue abilities. Catching negative thought patterns early allows for replacing them with balanced self-talk and modifying behaviors accordingly. For example, replace "I always mess this up" with "I will learn as I go and improve" or "No one knows as much as I do" with "My perspective is one of many worth considering." When confidence fluctuates, using supportive people with less emotional investment for practical feedback can keep perspectives in check.

Finally, finding confidence means striking a careful balance between acknowledging limitations and potential without diminishing either. It accepts imperfection gracefully and believes in continual growth, stronger than any single moment of uncertainty. Maintaining perspective through ups and downs serves relationships well by conveying flexibility, teachability, and care for mutual understanding over being completely right. Ultimate confidence emerges from within but flourishes through cooperation, not arrogance or self-doubt alone.

The Psychological Foundations of Self-Confidence

Self-confidence emerges from a variety of life experiences that shape our perceptions, starting at a young age. Factors within relationships, environmental influences, and personal accomplishments all serve to cultivate either assurance or doubt within an individual as character forms over time. Some foundational elements that contribute significantly to the development of one's belief in oneself include supportive relationships, achievement and feedback, and resilience in the face of challenges.

Warm, encouraging interactions help lay the groundwork. Children who feel seen, heard, and celebrated for their efforts through attentive parenting and mentors tend to carry that affirmation into later years. Peer bonds, where one feels accepted for who they are, also play a role. Conversely, those subjected to frequent criticism or lacking close allies can internalize negativity.

Achievements, no matter their scale, serve to reinforce the messages of influencers by allowing direct experience of competence. From learning to tie shoes to earning an advanced degree, overcoming hurdles through perseverance reminds us that continued effort often leads somewhere. It's crucial that our feedback serves to guide rather than discourage, as praise balances any corrections by acknowledging progress, too. In this light, setbacks teach resilience over regret.

Belief in self-determination, the ability to impact outcomes, shields from feelings of inadequacy compared to others. Trusting oneself as the author of one's circumstances lets confidence rise internally instead of relying on external validation. Self-driven goals provide a measuring stick for continuous development rather than perfection. Having sponsors along the journey to shore up efforts sustains forward momentum.

Inevitably, life will bring stressors, but confidence born from the stable foundations of supportive bonds, small wins, and resilience allows one to roll with life's complexities. A flexible perspective reminds us that challenges pose opportunities for personal growth just as much as the risk of failure. An inner assurance that more exists within than current conditions makes brighter days seem attainable.

Practical Strategies for Developing Self-Confidence

Having explored self-confidence's developmental foundations, attention now turns to proactive ways of strengthening this asset. While circumstance plays a role, research shows belief in oneself heavily depends on mindset and involvement in confidence-boosting behaviors. Small adjustments taken consistently can support more positive self-perceptions that become ingrained over the long run.

Recognize your own accomplishments, however modest they seem. Make it a regular habit to journal three things you did well each day, from cooking a meal skillfully to having a productive work meeting. At the same time, it is also important to reflect on past successes when feeling discouraged. This shifts focus to achievements versus fixating on flaws.

Speak to yourself with as much care as you would a friend. Negative self-talk undercuts hard work, while encouragement energizes further progress. Noting automatic critical thoughts helps replace them with supporters like "I'm learning." Talking positively to others reinforces kindness towards yourself, too.

Set stretch goals that excite rather than stress. With short-term aims coming in manageable steps, larger aspirations feel attainable through perseverance rather than intimidation. Weekly progress reviews keep plans feeling empowering instead of overwhelming as mastery grows.

Put energy into relationships where you receive empathy and support in return. Surrounding yourself with people invested in mutual care helps drown out unconstructive voices and brings out your best qualities. Confidence comes from within, but being valued by close ones strengthens it.

Try new activities that invite slight discomfort to expand comfort zones gradually. From conversational meetups to adventure outings, stepping outside routines and pushing limits a bit at a time builds confidence in adapting to change. The new skills acquired further reinforce self-assurance. Express gratitude for abilities and situations. Taking time each evening to identify and record some things one is thankful for shifts focus to abundance while also boosting mood and relationships. Contentment breeds more confidence than a continual desire for more.

How Self-Belief Boosts Well-Being

"The way you treat yourself sets the standard for others."
— Sonya Friedman

Having invested in personal growth and cultivating assurance from within, individuals start to experience an enhanced quality of life through many channels. Confidence lifts performance, strengthens relationships, fosters learning, and boosts overall health and happiness. Such benefits reinforce the continued commitment to sustaining self-belief as a priority.

When we trust in ourselves, stress and self-doubt diminish focus, so energy shifts outward to achieve goals. Believing in preparation and staying composed under pressure allows performing abilities to reach higher levels. Confidence to tackle challenges brings out greater potential that wouldn't emerge through fear and avoidance.

Interactions turn more positive as confidence promotes self-assured communication and active listening. People feel at ease around those comfortable in their own skin. Close relationships experience less volatility from insecurity, while respect and trust grow stronger. Leadership skills come naturally as assured guidance energizes others.

Eliminating hesitation in taking risks cultivates a growth mindset, thriving on feedback and learning from both failures and successes.

Perspective remains open to improvement versus discouragement, so stress levels stay reasonable. Awareness that setbacks arise from experience, not personal flaws, keeps progress enjoyable through challenges.

Physical and mental health benefit immensely, as assurance provides a protective buffer from life's uncertainties. The stress response stays balanced, energy is higher, and mood is more stable in the long term. Self-care comes naturally with intrinsic self-worth rather than seeking worth only externally through constant approval-seeking or comparison.

Overall satisfaction arises from within through self-belief in one's abilities to craft a meaningful path. While circumstances may change, confidence anchors internal resilience through transitions. Accomplishments feel all the sweeter when trusting one's capacity for change and overcoming struggles with perseverance and flexibility.

So, in cultivating self-confidence lie tremendous rewards, not just for goals achieved alone but also for maximizing potential, maintaining wellness, and finding overall purpose and joy in life's journey. Continued focus on building belief propels growth both personally and in relationships with others to higher planes. Truly, confidence unlocks doors to a quality of life difficult to attain otherwise.

CHAPTER 8

ENHANCING SOCIAL SKILLS

"Empathy and social skills are social intelligence, the interpersonal part of emotional intelligence; that's why they look alike."

-Daniel Goleman

Social skills are an important part of how we interact with one another. The small interactions we have each day, whether at work, school, or among friends and family, require us to understand how to relate to others and navigate different social situations. While it may seem simple for some, social skills can be challenging for many people to learn and master.

This is why focusing on social skills from a young age and continuously working to strengthen them throughout life is so beneficial. Our modern, technology-driven world provides many convenient methods of communication, but it also threatens to weaken the social exchanges that humans have practiced for millennia. For example, excessive time spent engaging with screens reduces opportunities to build social skills through face-to-face interactions where nuanced body language, facial expressions, and tone of voice aid understanding.

Interpersonal communication is about so much more than just the words themselves. Developing keen observational abilities and learning to read between the lines of what others say helps us understand varying perspectives. It fosters empathy, allowing us to consider how our own actions or viewpoints might affect others. Strong social skills also improve our ability to analyze group dynamics and handle challenging social situations tactfully. This results in fewer missed opportunities for collaboration or allays potential conflicts before they arise.

Beyond professional and academic success, social skills positively impact our personal relationships and overall well-being. People with highly developed interpersonal skills report higher life satisfaction and healthier coping methods. Close relationships act as a support system and buffer against feelings of loneliness or isolation, which research links to increased risks for various mental and physical health issues. Even simple social encounters, like smiling at a cashier or greeting neighbors when outside, can help fulfill our inherent need for human connection and community.

On the other hand, a lack of social skills often stems from anxiety about social judgments or difficulty reading social cues. But with time and practice, most anyone can strengthen their skills. A few tried strategies include joining local clubs or activity groups involving interests you enjoy. This creates low-pressure social situations. Observing how others interact also proves beneficial for recognizing social norms. Try roleplaying various scenarios with a close friend's help to build confidence in your abilities. And remember, mistakes may happen, so focus on kindness toward yourself as well as others when practicing.

The value of social skills becomes apparent when considering the lifelong repercussions of poor development in this area during childhood or adolescence. While intelligence quotient (IQ) plays a role in many outcomes, research indicates social-emotional competence largely predicts academic performance, career attainment, and the quality of relationships even more strongly. Individuals with subpar social skills tend to encounter greater unemployment, earn less income, and face poorer physical and psychological health over their lifetime. Some may require social skills training later in life.

Ultimately, we are social creatures who depend on one another. Strong communication abilities and emotional intelligence help communities function, businesses progress, and countries thrive. On an individual level, adequate social skills ensure fuller participation in society while safeguarding personal well-being and happiness. With patient focus on strengthening these skills, anyone can achieve socially and professionally fulfilling lives ahead. When viewed as an investment for the future rather than a short-term task, developing social competence becomes a priority worth ongoing commitment throughout each stage of life.

The Hidden Repercussions of Poor Social Skills

As established, social skills play a crucial role in navigating life's various opportunities and challenges. However, beyond the academic, career, and health ramifications already noted, insufficiently developed social skills can inflict other subtler costs with their own long-lasting effects, though these risks are sometimes difficult to recognize.

Those lacking social confidence may shrink from experiences that expand perspectives and foster empathy. They might avoid classes, activities, and environments, exposing them to diverse groups of people. While intended as a short-term comfort, this social withdrawal has unintended downsides. Isolation breeds narrow-mindedness and deficits in understanding human complexity, which society increasingly demands in a multicultural world. It also ties into worsening mental health risks over time, such as depression.

Avoiding social discomfort denies chances to build resilience. Learning how to overcome awkward interactions or put ourselves in unfamiliar situations benefits psychological flexibility, even when anxiety arises. This allows us to roll with life's unpredictability instead of reacting strongly to changes beyond our control. Those with poor social skills have not built a tolerance for ambiguity or learned from small failures, missing out on the confidence that results.

Subpar social abilities further influence relationship quality, career success, and community involvement in more subtle ways. Strained friendships and romance may discourage pursuing happiness through close bonds. Few social supports increase workplace fatigue and reduce job satisfaction, impacting long-term retention and productivity. With fewer natural public speaking opportunities from hobbies or classes, the fear of presentations at work remains.

Individuals may also miss opportunities to make positive impacts through social activism, mentorship programs, and leadership roles. Weak social skills preclude involving others to address real-world issues through collaborative group efforts. Societies lose out on untapped talents when capable citizens remain on the sidelines due to a lack of networking or social ease.

With diligence, of course, anyone can strengthen these "soft" life skills throughout life. However, recognizing their underrated yet wide-ranging benefits provides strong motivation to start small. By embracing social-skill building as a long-haul investment offering numerous rewards, individuals can avoid negative experiences that sometimes only emerge in hindsight.

"Our emotions need to be as educated as our intellect. It is important to know how to feel, how to respond, and how to let life in so that it can touch you."

— Jim Rohn

Practical Ways to Enhance Your Social Skills

Now that we've explored the extensive value yet also subtle risks of underdeveloped social skills, the discussion turns hopeful. Many approaches exist for anyone seeking strategies to bolster their abilities in this crucial life domain, requiring only small initial steps. Patience, persistence, and treating occasional discomforts or mishaps along the way with self-kindness prove most effective.

One proven method involves consciously broadening social circles by seeking out low-pressure environments. Community centers often host enjoyable, low-cost activities and classes that expose you to like-minded people, from craft or language classes to sports. You need not converse deeply, but you can benefit from observing others' interactions. Libraries likewise provide programs, as do clubs matching passions for history, games, or hobbies. Enjoying activities together naturally sparks shared conversation topics.

For greater challenges inducing social anxiety, enlisting an understanding friend's assistance can help. With a patient buddy, roleplaying upcoming situations like parties, meetings, or presentations calms jitters and builds confidence through practice. Switching roles provides a unique perspective on your own behaviors and impacts. Keep roleplays positive, focusing on strengths.

Daily habits also shape social skills in the long term. Even in passing, initiating small talk and friendliness with clerks or neighbors satisfies the fundamental need for connection while easing you into practicing comfort among strangers. Smiling warmly and making eye contact dramatically improve first impressions. Journaling about social experiences allows for reflected learning from each interaction, pattern, or emotion felt.

Mastering active listening shows care and respect for others. Summarizing what people share and asking open-ended questions keeps discussions lively yet makes the speaker feel heard. Compliments, when given thoughtfully and sparingly, brighten days without empty flattery. And remember, among valued friends, even an occasional faux pas likely won't damage bonds of mutual understanding and support.

By applying these every-day suggestions and steadily facing the challenges patience provides, anyone can enhance their social skills step-by-step. Building resilience and relationships simultaneously boosts overall well-being and opens future opportunities, bringing rewards in both the personal and professional realms for years ahead.

The Many Advantages of Strong Social Skills

So far, we've examined social skills from an intellectual perspective, exploring their underlying mechanics, role in healthy psychosocial development, and techniques for strengthening areas that need work. However, a balanced discussion would be remiss without emphasizing the concrete dividends strong social skills can pay in real-world living. While not guaranteed, statistics show cultivating these abilities through diligent practice is often associated with notable life benefits well worth cultivating.

Relationally, the upside, perhaps most vital to personal happiness, involves deeper, longer-lasting friendships and relationships. Those socially comfortable exploring various groups tend to enjoy larger support networks, bolstering wellness. Their partners also report higher relationship satisfaction, aided by strong communication skills and resolving conflicts respectfully. Close friends can offer perspectives beyond one's own bubble while cushioning stressful periods with dependable shoulders.

Socially proficient people likewise access broader opportunities. Whether recreational, social sports, volunteer committees, professional conferences, or community boards, plentiful activities welcome new members - those willing and able to interact positively with others. Such settings expand worldviews through fresh ideas while highlighting untapped talents seldom noticeable to introverted personalities. Diverse connections boost career options through references aware of one's work.

Statistics suggest socially adept employees receive higher salaries, bonuses, and positive reviews over time. Their work relationships prove durable while sparing workplace tensions. Presentation and small-talk abilities during meetings, brainstorming, or networking events benefit strategic career moves. Leaders note that smooth cooperation flows from staff and that interpersonal diplomacy is smoothly navigated. Many companies prioritize "soft skills" when recruiting and retaining versatile talent, contributing positively to team dynamics.

Mental resilience also emerges from facing the challenges of novel social situations with poise. Overcoming awkwardness makes one a flexible problem-solver adept at change navigation. Self-confidence permeating social domains transitions readily into other areas of life. Physical well-being may further rise with broader engagement, counteracting inflammation linked to loneliness. Laughter and cheer exuded through strong social skills spread infectious goodwill.

While not easily measurable, social skills remain one vital talent that liberates people to their greatest potential. Their numerous lifetime advantages make effort invested in building these abilities both a present and future-oriented choice always worthy of pursuit.

CHAPTER 9

COMMUNICATING EFFECTIVELY

"If you just communicate, you can get by. But if you communicate skillfully, you can work miracles."

– Jim Rohn,

Communication is something we all take part in every single day, whether it's chatting with family, coordinating at work, or simply posting online. Yet it's easy to overlook just how much power our ability to communicate holds.

We live in an incredibly connected world where endless messages, updates, and conversations are constantly being exchanged. But it wasn't always this way. For most of humanity, sharing ideas, news, or stories over long distances has been very difficult. People in one community would have little knowledge about what was happening even just a few miles away. It's amazing to think about how profoundly technology has altered the communication landscape in only a few short generations. Compared to any other time in history, we are now connected on a truly global scale like never before.

This new connectivity spanning the entire planet has untold positive effects but also reveals how reliant we have become on seamless communication in our daily lives. The simplest tasks that we take for granted, from arranging a meeting to getting directions, accessing information, or staying in touch with friends, lean heavily on the infrastructure that facilitates interaction across vast networks. A disruption to any part of this system would have wide-reaching consequences. During times when services fail or networks go down, even briefly, it highlights the integral role that communication plays in powering modern society.

Yet, for all its benefits, our constant connectivity also causes information overload if not managed properly. We are presented with more news, opinions, and updates than any one person could reasonably process on their own. As a result, the ability to sift through massive amounts of content and focus only on what's truly important or relevant has become a valuable skill. For some, constant updates can induce anxiety about always being "plugged in." Thus, moderation and balance hold equal importance.

The discussion makes clear that, for good or ill, communication abilities now underpin almost everything we do from day to day. How efficiently and thoughtfully we share, spread, and utilize information will continue to shape our communities and world at a rapid pace into the future. Maintaining open lines of communication and focusing on thoughtful, fact-based discussion is key amid so much online chatter. In that sense, we each play an active role in either further empowering communication for humankind's benefit or allowing it to sow discord. The power of communication ultimately lies in how we each choose to wield and spread ideas.

The Significance of Meaningful Communication

While the power of communication itself is immense, it's important to recognize that not all communication is equally impactful. For information to have value and truly connect people, it must be delivered effectively. This begins with carefully considering how, when, and where a message will be conveyed. Strategic planning helps ensure communication is productive rather than counterproductive or misunderstood.

Clarity of expression is important because we all interpret things through our unique lenses of experience and biases. No matter the topic, the sender's expertise level, or how brilliant an idea may seem, it will fall flat or even undermine the intended purpose if not communicated skillfully. Taking the time to organize ideas in a logical flow, define any necessary terms, and consider the reader's perspective can make all the difference in engaging an audience and having real influence.

An additional key factor is choosing methods of communication appropriate for both the message and the people receiving it. While digital platforms may seem ideal for broad reach, sometimes a phone call or in-person meeting better conveys nuance or builds necessary rapport. Too many options can fragment focus, so focus is crucial. Likewise, consideration for others involves selecting channels they prefer and will engage with fully, rather than disregarding them.

Equally important is listening effectively. Truly understanding others often means less talking and more carefully taking in multiple viewpoints. Both parties are listening for understanding rather than just reflexively formulating a response and cultivating an environment where people feel heard and well-represented. Such engagement fosters meaningful dialogue more than any monologue ever could.

Thoughtfully weighing all these factors of clear expression, matching method to message and audience, and elevating listening as much as speaking—that is what makes communication most powerful and fruitful. Meaning emerges from harmonizing all parties around shared understanding rather than just disseminating isolated facts. When done right, communication has the potential to positively transform situations in a way that leaves people feeling brought together instead of pushed apart.

The Impact of Communication on Our Relationships

Our personal and professional lives center greatly around relationships with others, whether at home or at work. As social creatures, we're wired for connection. However, building and maintaining strong relationships takes consistent effort. Effective communication plays a vital supporting role.

In our private lives, openly discussing feelings, listening without judgment, and compromising when needed are hallmarks of healthy communication between partners, family, and friends. Misunderstandings are unavoidable at times, but addressing issues respectfully and prioritizing each other's perspectives preserves intimacy and trust in the long run. Those who communicate their fears or needs clearly, rather than stewing in silence, end up feeling more secure in their bonds.

Similarly, the workplace depends on cooperation between coworkers pursuing shared goals. People can stay coordinated and productive even during demanding periods by sharing status updates, brainstorming ideas together constructively, and giving thoughtful feedback. Those who communicate proactively, ask questions to clarify, and explain rationales persuasively tend to face fewer frustrations and resolve conflicts smoothly. Collaboration thrives when information flows freely within teams tackling complex problems.

However, personal lives inform professional conduct as much as vice versa. Being aware of nonverbal cues, maintaining appropriate boundaries, and providing sensitive support are hallmarks of healthy office dynamics. Allowing personal issues to undermine interactions risks damaging morale and focus. Role models who communicate consistently with care, empathy, and accountability earn broad respect and leadership over time.

With practice and reflection on both verbal and nonverbal aspects, we can strengthen communication skills to nurture relationships of all kinds. Thoughtful communication plays a major role in determining individual success as well as the greater welfare of any community we're part of, whether family, workplace, or broader social circles. Our relationships are one of life's greatest gifts, and effective communication safeguards that gift.

The Pitfalls of Ineffective Communication

While the importance of meaningful communication is abundantly clear, it's also crucial to acknowledge the very real drawbacks that arise from weak communication skills. Poor communication practices can breed significant frustration and wasted effort over time for both individuals and the organizations they're part of. Recognizing these downsides helps emphasize the value of continuously improving one's abilities.

A lack of clarity often stems from communication troubles, as messages are either misunderstood or misinterpreted altogether due to imprecise wording, content disorganization, or failure to define key terms. This can cause confusion, mistaken assumptions, and rework as the true intent becomes muddled or hidden between the lines. For projects, a lack of shared understanding and timely updates can easily lead to lost efficiency and coordination issues that snowball.

The source and flow of information also matter tremendously. Withholding necessary details or failing to properly listen to others' perspectives means important context never surfaces to inform decisions. This breeds insularity, whereas freely sharing information across teams cultivates collaborative problem-solving and fresh ideas being explored from multiple angles. When members don't feel heard or that ideas can be shared candidly, innovation and motivation may start to decline within that environment over time.

Unaddressed communication breakdowns will invariably undermine relationships and create disconnects if allowed to persist. Miscommunications left unresolved leave lingering doubts and hard feelings that damage trust when they resurface later. Poor conflict management exacerbates problems rather than bringing resolution. Both personal and professional relationships depend on regular, clear, and constructive exchanges to sustain meaningful connections.

All in all, strong communication skills must be honed consciously and applied diligently to avoid the frequent pitfalls caused by their absence. Prioritizing effective speaking, active listening, comprehension, and coordination enables people and organizations alike to perform at higher levels on a consistent basis.

Ways to Strengthen Communication Skills

While communication issues can certainly hinder relationships and productivity if left unaddressed, the good news is that these skills can also be continuously refined through practice and self-reflection. No one is born an expert communicator, and room for growth exists for all of us in these abilities. However, prioritizing communication development opens doors to improved personal and professional lives for ourselves and those around us.

For many, giving structured thought to how they interact can spark insights to apply going forward. Taking time to analyze where discussions tend to stall, or relationships face obstacles reveals habits to consciously improve upon. Learning to view exchanges and information-sharing efforts from others' perspectives helps us connect more understandingly. Recording ourselves can also expose unhelpful verbal tics or how cues like facial expressions and body language enhance or diminish spoken points.

Actively listening, without internally planning a rebuttal during another's reply, honors their perspective and ensures we truly understand each other. Asking respectful questions for clarity and repeating our interpretations allows the speaker to also confirm comprehension. In return, being conscious of concise yet thorough explanations of our own viewpoints models effective communication for others to reference.

Ongoing education also strengthens communication abilities through reading recommendations, online courses, or in-person workshops focused on public speaking, conflict mediation, or even productive work discussions. Establishing regular feedback frameworks within relationships or professional settings further cultivates a growth mindset, as we sincerely aim to meet others' needs through our interactions.

With application comes reward, as these best practices become ingrained habits. Employing various techniques appreciates that each person and situation differs, requiring adaptability. However, a shared goal of understanding one another can bring out the best in all relationships through strengthened communication.

The Rewards of Effective Communication

After examining the potency of communication and how proper skills can be built over time, it is worthwhile to reflect on the positive outcomes that result from such efforts. When communication channels operate smoothly and people feel their viewpoints are understood, it creates a fertile environment where many benefits naturally emerge.

Relationships at all levels deepen substantially as mutual understanding grows. Connections between friends, family, and coworkers take on new meaning when ideas can be candidly shared, and empathy comes easier through active listening. Few things bring people closer than the intimacy of conveying hearts and minds fully without concern for judgment or a need to force compliance. Partners or teams that communicate this way tend to weather challenges with the united support of one another.

In the workplace, stronger communication fosters higher productivity and more innovative solutions being found collaboratively. Clients and managers alike develop confidence in those who interact clearly and work effectively with others to complete projects on schedule. Conveying updates promptly leaves little room for assumptions to form. With information flowing freely and obstacles addressed head-on, stress levels stay manageable even during busy periods.

The resulting increase in cooperation, cohesion, and job satisfaction that comes from polished communication skills has profound flow-on effects. Organizations benefit from more engaged, dedicated employees who feel empowered as contributors rather than replaceable cogs. Professionals with reputations for listening with empathy and conveying perspectives persuasively find themselves leading productive discussions that move an organization forward by leaps and bounds over time.

On a personal growth level, communication development cultivates emotional intelligence as we learn to understand diverse viewpoints. It boosts confidence to know interactions are undergirded by respect, clarity, and diplomacy. Rare is the career path or social circle that does not require this crucial competence. Realizing relationships and opportunities are what give life its fullest rewards, strengthening our communication abilities pays a lifetime of dividends.

CHAPTER 10

CULTIVATING RESILIENCE

"Resilience is not about bouncing back but about rising strong, learning from adversity, and growing into someone even more capable of handling life's challenges."

-Anonymous

We all face challenges in life, from small hardships to significant setbacks. How we weather difficulties and continue to grow is uniquely personal. Some reflect upon resilience, but true strength comes from within, not metrics or comparisons.

Each experience shapes us. With time and perspective, insights often emerge. During trying times, certain traits like persistence, adaptability, and community can buoy our spirits. But we are complex beings; what sustains one may drain another.

Rather than judgment, self-understanding needs compassion. Have we avoided pain at the cost of disconnecting from life's richness? Do we embrace each moment fully, good and bad alike? Our answers will likely change as circumstances do.

Our limits are as human as our potential. When we accept this, pressure lifts, and we can support one another through highs and lows, celebrate small victories, and recall that our shared hopes outweigh hard days. Each walking their own path teaches what really matters—connections forming as we walk together.

Life rewards those who meet each other each day with open and forgiving hearts. As we reflect on resilience, may we do so to find empathy—for ourselves and all those traveling similar roads. Our journeys continue as long as we embrace each moment's lessons, however deep or simple they may seem, with caring for ourselves and others as our guide.

Making Time For Reflection

Our daily lives can feel overwhelmingly busy at times. Between work responsibilities, family commitments, social obligations, and everything else filling our schedules, it's easy to feel constantly pulled in a hundred directions without pause. Yet in the midst of this active whirlwind, it is so important that we make time for quieter moments of stillness and reflection as well. Checking in with ourselves without tasks or deadlines as a focus, allows an opportunity to nurture self-awareness that can be overlooked in more frenetic times.

Taking even 10 or 15 minutes a day to simply sit quietly offers a chance to become more present with our thoughts and feelings. Whether it happens first thing in the morning with a cup of tea, during lunch amid the work day's bustle, or before bed as we unwind from the evening, those brief periods of calm presence can do much for our wellbeing. It allows a shift away from our active "to-do" mindset, instead opening us up to thoughtful awareness of how our mind, body, and spirit are feeling in that moment. In that stillness, we might notice aspects of daily life we've been racing through without much reflection.

Such time for reflection without demands upon it can serve as a sort of emotional check-in, leaving us feeling more centered and able to engage fully with whatever tasks and relationships we turn to next. That reflective pause may reveal more things we need, like joy, rest, or human connection. Or it might point us towards underlying stresses, changes we want to make, or even small daily joys we have been taking for granted. The benefits resonate greatly, helping us strengthen our understanding of ourselves. Overall, allowing that regular moment of calm reflection amid rushing lives nourishes self-awareness in ways that can dramatically improve our wellbeing and strengthen resilience in facing challenges that come our way, both large and small.

Recalling Challenges Faced

All of us encounter struggles throughout our lives, whether great difficulties or small hardships that come up along the way. As we reflect with an open mind, it allows us to gain a clearer insight into our strengths as well as life's enduring lessons. Though remembering past pain can stir up difficult emotions, deeper wisdom lies in how we have navigated challenges and continued moving forward.

Perhaps you've experienced failures that seemed like crushing blows at the time. With perspective, recognize that these setbacks need not define you; each also likely reveals an underlying determination or heart that will serve you well in future endeavors. Relationships may have changed or ended in sorrow, yet the love within survives. Illnesses, injuries, or losses touch our lives in ways not always fair, yet within each remains our shared humanity—we all rise together through shared compassion.

Rather than solely focusing on the troubles themselves, reflect through a warmer lens on what it took within you to persevere. Traits like resilience, compassion for oneself and others, or simply continuing each day may seem like small victories now, but they show a resilient spirit. Know too that every difficulty, as every joy, connects us; our capacity for empathy fuels hope that we can walk together, supporting one another.

Life's difficulties, though painful, inform our character but do not dictate it. There remains light ahead in each new day and the chance to help others see it, too. Recall past struggles not to dwell in hurt but to appreciate every lesson and laugh that led you here, better equipped to lift each other with patience, gratitude, and care for one another. Our shared experience is proof enough that light perseveres.

Focusing On Feelings

When reflecting thoughtfully on past hardships, it can be insightful to tune inward and check in with how we truly feel about those experiences. Surface emotions provide valuable clues about our resilient qualities and areas in which to nurture self-care further. However, this inward look requires gentleness rather than critical assessment.

Recalling prior difficulties naturally brings up a variety of feelings: sadness, pride, regret, or relief. Note with kindness how your emotions lean rather than make strict tallies. Did perseverance through challenges leave you feeling strengthened, or did facing struggles in isolation cause feelings of being overwhelmed? Both resilience traits and areas of vulnerability likely resided within your responses, as well as within us all.

The purpose here is to gain self-awareness and not pass judgment on yourself or deny any part of the varied human experience. If guilt or shame creeps in around past responses, meet those feelings with patient reassurance rather than inner criticism. Your capability to feel such emotions, as with all others, is simply part of being human—a reminder that within each experience exist both lessons learned and room for growth.

Through this reflective process with a softened gaze, greater clarity on your character likely emerges naturally. Focus on recognizing the effort applied, not on perceiving any "right" way of handling struggles. With self-acceptance comes the freedom to set future goals aligned with your well-being, rather than out of a need to measure up to imagined standards that breed self-doubt. May this practice nurture your resilient spirit even more through compassion.

Observing Body Reactions

When reflecting on challenging periods in our lives, our bodies often hold subtler responses worth exploring with an open and understanding perspective. How does simply recalling certain difficulties or uncertainties from the past feel within your physical being? Are muscles tightening or thoughts becoming muddled—signs perhaps pointing to areas where more inner peace may still be found?

Take notice of embodied reactions gently, without harsh interpretation. A dizzying mind or tense shoulders do not equate to personal flaws but rather show where care and nurturing are most needed presently. Our resilient spirits are not measured by an absence of stress responses, which naturally arise at times for all people, but by how we use them as insights to strengthen self-understanding and compassion.

If distressing memories leave you feeling on edge physically, this prompts you to look inward with care toward your emotional, mental, and social wellbeing just as much as outward fixes. Regular relaxing activities become especially vital - through soothing hobbies, peaceful surroundings, comforting relationships, or even conscious breathing practices to unwind tightness wherever it is held.

With the same softness extended to yourself as you would a dear friend in need, acknowledge such reactions for the important messages they carry rather than as imperfections to dismiss or dislike. Their presence illustrates an opportunity to stoke resiliency's nourishing flames through moments of calm, joy, hope, and solidarity each day. Our highest strength arises from accepting ourselves and each other in full.

Considering Support Systems

Within each challenge, a solid support system bolsters our ability to endure while growing ever stronger. Indeed, positive relationships prove a reservoir of resilience that we all do well to tend throughout our journeys together. As social beings, we thrive through reciprocity—the giving and receiving of care, understanding, and affection.

In reflection, take stock of the trusted people in your life, both near and far. Do fulfilling bonds exist where you feel truly known and accepted without pretense? Does the current of care flow in two ways, with mutual listening to lift each other's burdens in a balanced measure? Or have stresses left you insulating, depriving all, including yourself, of the solace found within the community?

No one can walk alone. Thus, we must make conscious efforts to fill our lives with compassionate souls. But relationships, too, demand selflessness - for however much support you receive, look inward as well to ensure the tap flows in reverse, too. In dark moments, are you open in distress or found giving aid when others falter? A resilient spirit knows life's hardships shared halve their load, while joy doubles in company.

All can benefit from this retrospective check on connections, then work on strengthening bonds of reciprocity and care wherever strengthening may be needed. For those most trusted, they are the steady pillars able to uphold us over life's rocky terrain, allowing growth in tough times that forges resilience of the strongest kind. With community, we ride each twist and turn on wings of empathy.

Thinking About Self-Care

In addition to reflecting on relationships, taking stock of how well our lives nourish well-being on an individual level is important. Regular actions like restful sleep, nutritious eating, and creative leisure can fortify our capacity to handle challenges that come our way with grace and perseverance. As we care for loved ones, we must direct that same understanding inward toward self-nurturing.

Think about whether self-care routines feel balanced and restorative or if stresses sometimes pull focus. Consider whether sleep and fuel for our bodies promote sustained energy or if relaxation is scarce. Likewise, do activities just for enjoyment's sake spice life with moments of absorbed fun and meaning outside of daily duties? Paying heed ensures downtime replenishes the spirit as fully as a good night's sleep or meal does for the body.

If, at times, self-care slips lower on priorities, meet that with compassion as you would a friend. We are all humans, and life brings busy seasons. But do what feels right to restore equilibrium, whether earlier nights, a walk in nature, or calling a friend simply to laugh—things feeding the creative soul and relaxing the mind with no end goal but present living.

By making space for nourishing activities, we safeguard wellsprings of positivity that serve us well in facing difficulties. With the same warmth we show others, honor your valid needs, too. Only then can a resilient spirit and zest for life continue to thrive through whatever experiences each day may bring. May self-care find a balanced and consistent root so that you, in turn, can spread its uplifting fruits more widely.

Accepting Each Step

This inward glance we've taken provides a helpful perspective, but true self-understanding evolves gradually through life, just as we do. Beating ourselves up for perceived shortcomings serves no purpose, as does comparing our strengths and needs to unrealistic benchmarks. What matters is the continued walking of this path with patience, recognizing that growth happens in gentle increments over time.

Note new understandings that surface with care, just as insights into qualities already serving you well amid challenges. This balanced view builds self-esteem, not undermines it. And let motivation stem from a desire to better know and nurture yourself rather than checking items off a checklist; your well-being's deepest care emerges from within, from your own loving hand.

It must also be noted that resilience, like life itself, weaves no straight lines but spirals. Some days, our ability to adapt, find joy, or ask for aid comes with more ease, while others do not. None are static, and that flux is natural. As the seasons change, so do our needs and capacities. Trust that you possess the inner wisdom to face whatever comes and the skills to learn when facing difficulties anew.

With this reflective journey, view not an endpoint but a deepening of self-care, compassion for yourself and others traveling similarly, and gratitude for each step, no matter how small. In that lighter perspective lies freedom. May you thus feel emboldened to meet each challenge and moment with ever more understanding, acceptance, and care for your wonderful, complex self. Our shared humanity thrives best when nurtured.

The kindest evaluation is a changed perspective leading to more care for ourselves and compassion for life's shared human experiences. May reflection inspire patience and joy.

Cultivating Resilience Through Everyday Living

Self-reflection provides insights, but true resilience emerges through small yet meaningful actions integrated into daily life. As with plants nourished by regular water and sunlight, our ability to withstand difficulties and continue growing is cultivated over time through consistent, compassionate self-care.

Make supportive relationships a priority. Check in regularly with trusted friends and family, and prioritize quality time together. Strong bonds fuel resilience by allowing us to both give and receive help during tougher periods. Practice self-compassion. Meet challenges with patience and kindness, as you would a dear friend in need. Harsh self-criticism only breeds stress, where you can lighten obligations and affirm your inherent worth.

- Engage in activities for pleasure, whether hobbies, creativity, or appreciation for simple natural beauty. Leisure renews our enthusiasm for life.
- Ensure adequate rest. Health depends on regular, restorative sleep and periods of stillness to recharge. Protect time for rest as fiercely as other responsibilities.
- Move your body. Exercise boosts mental well-being, from endorphins during activity to better sleep and stress responses afterward. Find forms of movement you enjoy.
- Eat nutritious, balanced meals. Fuel your body with energy and nutrients to support your well-being through each challenge. Avoid relying on stress eating or substances to cope.

With a nurturing approach to everyday living that focuses on balance, care for others, appreciation for life's gifts, and self-acceptance, resilience weaves its steady strength. Over time and with compassion, we can overcome whatever difficulties come our way.

The Benefits of Cultivating Resilience

Developing resilience through consistent self-nurturing brings many rewards that enhance our well-being and ability to thrive. Some of the key benefits include an increased ability to handle difficulties with patience and optimism, deeper self-awareness and care, stronger relationships, and an overall greater zest for life.

Facing challenges with resilience means we experience them as opportunities for growth rather than threats to our well-being. Adversity is inevitable, but a resilient spirit allows it to roll off our backs more easily while we learn and strengthen. This calmer outlook spares us undue stress and leads to wisdom over time.

Resilience stems from gaining clarity on who we are and what we truly need through compassionate reflection. This roots our sense of value beyond external factors, so crises do not destabilize our core happiness. Self-understanding with care empowers us to make choices aligned with our wellness.

Nurturing resilience involves prioritizing supportive connections and giving and receiving help liberally. These relationships provide a vital safety net that lifts burdens and spirits during trying periods. Conversely, depleted well-being damages relationships, so building resilience to protect bonds is crucial for joy and endurance.

Overall health and positivity thrive when we meet each day, challenge, and moment with balanced care for ourselves and empathy for others. A resilient spirit faces life with a full cup, contentment, and appetite for whatever each turning wheel may offer—be it laughter or lessons ahead. This energizing outlook is its own reward, making difficulties bearable and the richness of experience something to celebrate.

CHAPTER 11

HANDLING STRESS
AND PRESSURE

"Emotional intelligence teaches us that stress is not what happens to us, but how we respond to it. with awareness we can turn pressure into an opportunity for growth."

- Anonymous

This chapter mainly talks about some of the health risks that come from feeling too much stress and pressure. It explains that stress is the body's reaction when it senses something that needs attention, a change, or a demand. Some stress is normal and can even be useful, but problems start when the stress levels stay very high for a long period of time.

When people feel overwhelmed by things they must deal with, their body enters a "fight or flight" response without realizing it. This response releases hormones that were helpful for our ancestors in dangerous situations long ago, but now it often happens for less serious things like work, money issues, or family problems. If this response turns on too frequently from daily stresses, it leads to real health problems over time. Some examples are high blood pressure, heart disease, tummy troubles, and sleep issues.

It can also negatively affect our moods, causing anxiety, feeling sad, or burning out. Feeling unable to handle what's asked of you or like you have no control over the pressures also causes major stress. Overall, some stress in life is natural, but too much constant stress without ways to manage it tires out the body and mind. It notes that stress affects different jobs and stages of life uniquely as well.

Teachers, for example, deal with big workloads and overcrowded classrooms. They are responsible for how students do on tests and behavior problems, all while still having duties at home. Young workers just starting out may stress over student loans and unstable jobs as they try to prove themselves. New parents have the sudden responsibility of a baby, while caring for aging parents also brings about stress for older adults.

In wrapping up, it reiterates that what causes stress varies widely between people depending on their situation and ability to cope. However, exceeding a tolerable amount of unmanaged pressure over time will inevitably undermine health and happiness regardless. Therefore, learning effective coping strategies for reducing and handling stress levels better is significant for total well-being. The next section explores practical approaches for doing that.

Importance of Handling Pressure and Stress

Moving further, this chapter highlights why it is so crucial that we find healthy ways to manage the stress and pressures that we experience in life. As was mentioned previously, some level of stress is normal and inevitable. Our bodies have natural stress response systems designed to deal with short-term threats. However, it's when stress becomes prolonged and chronic with no adequate coping that it poses serious risks.

If we don't learn to handle our stress effectively, it takes a real toll on both our physical and mental health over time. Studies show that sustained high stress puts us at greater risk for numerous medical issues like high blood pressure, heart disease, ulcers, sleep problems, and other similar problems.

These health impacts wind up costing societies tremendously in rising healthcare expenditures. On a personal level, who wants to feel overwhelmed and burned out on a regular basis? Constantly feeling like we're juggling more than we can take away enjoyment from life.

Our mental health also deteriorates when we don't address what's causing us persistent stress. We're more prone to anxiety, depression, and burnout. Not taking care of our mental well-being can erode our overall happiness and life satisfaction. Problems at work or home tend to feel magnified when we're under continual pressure without relief. Relationships with friends and family can become strained if stress is left unchecked for too long.

Finding positive approaches to dealing with what weighs on our minds is important for maintaining a balanced lifestyle and perspective. If issues constantly gnaw at us without an outlet, it's hard to experience much quality of life or be present for those around us. Coping doesn't mean toughing things out or avoiding them; it's about gaining skills to thoughtfully work through problems healthily.

Luckily, there are many strategies we can draw from, like exercising, talking it out with loved ones, practicing relaxation, spending time in nature, and developing healthier thought patterns. Having an arsenal of tactics helps ensure we don't rely too heavily on any one method. The key is the commitment to taking care of ourselves through stressful times the same way we care for our physical body through proper nutrition and activity. Our minds and emotions deserve attention, too.

Overall, life presents opportunities as much as challenges, and our capacity for both is impacted by how we process and manage what weighs on us. Coping constructively paves the path forward, no matter what curveballs come our way, personally or collectively. Prioritizing our well-being gives us more room to survive and thrive during times of change, uncertainty, and overload. It's about living life fully rather than feeling its strains sabotage our joy and potential.

Coping Strategies for Handling Everyday Stressors

This section discusses an array of approaches we can employ to keep stress levels in check. When stress becomes chronic or excessive, it's important that we take action by incorporating different activities for the care of our mental health. Experimenting with options helps identify what works best for how we each process and release tension or worry. While no single method is a cure-all, maintaining a toolkit provides flexibility depending on circumstances.

Exercise is a very effective stress buster. Physical activity like walking, yoga, or sports releases endorphins that improve mood. It also serves as a distraction while helping burn through the physical buzz of adrenaline created by stress. Even light exercise provides benefits if that's all time allows. Spending time outdoors and taking in natural scenes like parks, beaches, or hiking trails also has relaxing qualities. Being in nature lowers blood pressure and eases mental fatigue.

Creative hobbies and pursuits we enjoy are stress-relieving, whether playing an instrument, gardening, board games, woodworking, or other hands-on projects. These provide fulfillment while taking our focus off our worries. Maintaining connections through real interaction also lends perspective and lifts spirits. Whether catching up with close friends, engaging in community activities, or spending quality moments with family, social interaction satisfies a basic human need and allows venting problems.

Mindfulness practices have gained popularity in recent years for their effectiveness in managing stress and anxiety and promoting overall well-being. At their core, mindfulness techniques help train us to live more in the present moment rather than being stuck in thoughts about the past or future. This allows tensions from daily life to have less of a hold on us. Various activities like meditation, prayer, journaling, and deep breathing cultivate inner stillness and can lower stress levels when incorporated regularly.

Meditation involves focusing full, non-judgmental attention on something specific, like the breath, bodily sensations, or a repeated word or phrase. Only focusing on the chosen anchor and letting other thoughts come and go helps disrupt worry patterns. Research shows even brief daily meditation can shrink the amygdala over time—the brain's threat center linked to stress and anxiety responses. Many find guided meditation apps or classes most supportive when starting a routine.

Prayer, for those of faith, has comparable benefits to meditation. It involves centering attention on God, a higher power, or centered spaciousness, however understood.

Expressing care, concerns, and gratitude through prayer connects us to calming perspectives beyond our daily minutiae. Like silently repeating a meaningful phrase in rhythm with breathing, mantra-style prayer also settles nerves. Making prayer or quiet reflection part of morning or evening routines anchors stress care into daily life.

Journaling offers deep benefits by providing an outlet for processing emotions, thoughts, and experiences. Writing openly about stress helps get revelations from swirling minds onto paper. This externalizes worries into a manageable form, lifting some burdens from the conscious mind. Reading through past entries also fosters insight into patterns and perspectives worth maintaining. While journaling isn't right for all temperaments, it cultivates self-awareness and releases stress for many through expressive writing.

Deep, conscious breathing practices are another effective tool. Taking breaths deep into the belly for 5–10 minutes with a focus on breath sensations disrupts fight or flight stress reactions. Setting aside brief periods to simply listen inward through comfortable inhalations and exhalations centers attention in a way conducive to perspective shifts. Breathwork can be done almost anywhere and lends quick calm when unexpected stresses hit.

Adopting mindfulness techniques requires commitment as a regular practice, yet simple techniques woven into daily habits provide a well-rounded way of navigating the strains of life while retaining inner balance. Multitasking is challenging, but simple mantras like "breathe, notice, and let go" remind us to stay present so we aren't consumed by whatever difficulties come our way. This goes quite far in reducing stress and promoting health.

While stress itself cannot always be avoided, developing go-to coping strategies builds resilience to roll with life's challenges instead of being bent under their weight. With patience and commitment, we empower ourselves with options for managing what inevitably arises while safeguarding our long-term health and happiness.

Benefits of Effectively Managing Stress and Pressure

This section highlights some important ways that learning to handle stress and pressure better can positively impact our lives. While stress is an unavoidable part of existence, how we choose to relate to and process what strains us makes all the difference. Finding suitable coping techniques grants us more control amid times of high demand or issues beyond our power.

Being proactive about stress care contributes greatly to improved physical wellbeing. Those who implement strategies see declines in anxiety, depression, and cardiovascular ailments over time. Conditions like hypertension, which quietly takes lives, can be warded off through regular de-stressing. Reduced health risks and visits to the doctor translate to cost savings, both personally and community-wide. *Who doesn't want more vibrance and vitality each day?*

With stress in better regulation, cloudy emotions don't dominate or halt us from living fully. We stay engaged because non-stop worry hasn't depleted our resilience. Relationships maintain strength without friction from constant tension overflow. Employers benefit from workers demonstrating poise over panic, even amidst deadlines. Quality family or couple bonding happens without stress-staining joy.

Work or student performance stays strong without being derailment by the daily hassles weighing others down. Tasks get completed on level ground without last-minute desperation that breeds mistakes. Confidence surges, recognizing that we hold the means for handling pressures instead of feeling battered by them. Stress-smart folks attract opportunities because calm, focus, and optimism signal someone worth investing in.

Overall, prioritizing stress management energizes each sphere of life. It's not about eliminating struggles completely but gaining mastery over how we relate to and tackle challenges. Sustained health, deeper ties, and empowerment—these rewards motivate continuing to learn and apply new coping techniques even as life changes. Handling stress saves more than just our well-being; it fortifies everything worthwhile we endeavor to build.

CHAPTER 12

MANAGING CONFLICT

"Conflict is inevitable, but emotional intelligence allows us to approach it with empathy, seek understanding, and transform it into a path toward deeper connections."
                                            - Dr. Kimberly Pinckney

The topic of how to properly address disagreements and disputes between individuals, groups, or organizations is an important life skill. Whether it's arguing with a family member, coworkers not seeing eye to eye, or countries going to war, resolving conflicts constructively is vital for peaceful cooperation and progress. One can take various approaches when faced with opposition, and understanding the best strategies is helpful for navigating these challenging interpersonal dynamics.

One method is to directly confront the issue or person you are in conflict with. This is sometimes called the "competing" style, which involves aggressively advocating for your position without considering others' perspectives. While taking a firm stance may feel satisfying at the moment, it often only escalates tensions and damages relationships. People tend to get defensive when feeling attacked, making compromise less likely. A competing approach can leave both sides feeling resentful and unwilling to find common ground.

An alternative is passive avoidance, where disagreements are not addressed and problems are ignored in the hope they will go away. However, unresolved conflicts rarely dissolve on their own and usually fester below the surface. Postponing discussions allows misunderstandings to multiply and bad feelings to intensify over time. Kicking the can down the road may cause short-term discomfort but does little to rebuild trust or come to a long-term agreement both sides find tolerable. Similarly, sweeping problems under the rug typically backfires in the end.

Most experts argue that the best strategy combines assertiveness about one's own views with empathy for others' perspectives. This cooperative or "collaborating" style aims for a win-win resolution where all feel heard, and needs are met as much as reasonably possible. It starts by actively listening to fully understand differing positions and then finding shared interests beneath surface disagreements. Compromises that offer give-and-take are crafted to satisfy mutual concerns, rather than one side dictating terms.

Resolving conflicts collaboratively takes patience and open-mindedness. Egos must be set aside to consider alternatives outside the initial asking positions. Creative problem-solving searches for integrated solutions of mutual benefit instead of one party dominating another. Disagreeing respectfully without attacking the other side's character helps keep discussions constructive rather than destructive. Compromise means all leave somewhat dissatisfied but return to cooperating in pursuit of their joint interests and goals.

With practice, collaboration can transform disputes into opportunities for strengthening relationships and gaining new insights. Shared understanding built through civil dialogue enables people to come to voluntary agreements that feel legitimate and fair to everyone involved. This cooperative strategy for conflict management tends to achieve more harmonious and durable long-term resolutions compared to aggressive advocacy alone or passive inaction. While requiring extra effort, a collaborative approach to disagreements ultimately benefits all parties more than escalating conflicts further through attacking, avoiding, or one-upping opponent positions. With an open and empathetic mindset, even intense disputes can evolve into cooperation and mutual understanding over time.

The Perils of Poor Conflict Management

Being unable to successfully address and resolve conflicts often has serious negative consequences that can seriously impact individuals and their groups. When disagreements are not dealt with constructively through cooperation and compromise, tensions have a tendency to fester and escalate over time in dysfunctional ways. Relationships become strained, resentment grows, and people take more polarized stances as they lose sight of shared interests beneath surface disagreements.

Productivity and teamwork suffer when colleagues are at odds and refuse to find mutually agreeable solutions. Workplaces experiencing high levels of conflict see lowered employee morale, increased turnover as people quit, and decreased customer satisfaction, which harms a business's bottom line. Similarly, personal conflicts that are not properly managed spill over and disrupt family functioning. Friends drift apart, children raised in high-conflict homes face developmental issues, and divorce or other breakdowns of social bonds are more likely without cooperation.

A lack of collaborative dispute resolution carries even graver threats when conflicts escalate into aggression, violence, or criminal activities between opposing sides. Some research indicates unaddressed workplace disputes can sometimes manifest in acts like sabotage, violence against coworkers, or even mass shootings by disgruntled former employees.

On a larger societal scale, tensions between cultural, ethnic, or ideological groups denied productive nonviolent means of reconciliation are prone to escalating into riots or insurgencies. History shows that without peaceful dispute settlement, even differences between nations risk dangerous military escalation and world wars.

The costs of not effectively dealing with inevitable disagreements, whether as individuals or within larger sectors of society, are simply too high to ignore. Burying our heads in the sand and hoping conflicts blow over on their own rarely succeeds long-term. While collaboration takes effort and flexibility, it remains far preferable to damaging alternatives that rip apart relationships and communities and even threaten global security.

With practice and open-mindedness, most disputes can transform into opportunities to deepen understanding, but only if all sides commit to managing disagreements through respect, active listening, and creative problem-solving instead of volatile reactions and avoidance. The alternative risks spiraling into fear, instability, and potentially catastrophic destruction if left unchecked.

Developing Strong Conflict Management Skills

Effectively handling disagreements, whether in personal or professional relationships, is an important life skill that can be developed with effort over time. While some people seem naturally adept at resolving conflicts, it requires learning healthy communication strategies and practicing collaborative problem-solving for most. Developing strong conflict management abilities allows one to navigate interpersonal difficulties in a productive manner and build stronger, happier bonds with others. Here are some approaches to enhancing this important competency:

Self-awareness is key; take time for introspection on your own conflict tendencies and triggers. Do you react angrily or get defensive easily? Understanding one's patterns of thought and behavior in stressful situations provides insight into how to avoid reactive responses. Having empathy for others' perspectives also helps, which can be increased through perspective-taking exercises.

Communication style is another important area of focus. Learn to separate people from problems when arguing, focusing on circumstances, not character. Attentive listening without judgment allows for understanding others thoroughly before being understood. Taking time to cool off if upset also prevents escalation. Nonviolent language lowers tensions by criticizing actions respectfully, not people.

Asserting needs to be done directly yet considerately to train cooperation over competition or avoidance. Compromise leaves people equally dissatisfied but committed to solving shared dilemmas collaboratively for mutual benefit instead of one side's demands alone. Brainstorming multiple solutions taps creative potentials unavailable to any individual alone.

Roleplaying disputes with trusted partners exercises these skills safely. Seeing how varied responses affect outcomes teaches moderating initial tone as well as finding synergistic resolutions where all parties feel ownership in solutions. Mediation experience resolving other people's conflicts transfers awareness to building agreements that satisfy everyone involved.

Learning sometimes means setting aside stubbornness to consider other perspectives with fresh lenses. Keeping cooperation and an empathetic understanding of others' humanity as the priority over "dominating" fosters improved relations even after immediate disputes have concluded. Education on conflicts recurring in society at large also guides the avoidance of their escalation elsewhere.

Ultimately, conflict resolution is an ongoing process of refining one's approach through experience navigating disagreements that will inevitably arise throughout life's challenges and changes. With dedicated development, handling difficulties as learning experiences rather than threats builds strong individual and shared capacities for positively transforming interpersonal tensions into cooperation.

The Many Advantages of Mastering Conflict Management

It may not always feel this way in the midst of heated disputes, but having well-developed conflict management abilities provides significant professional and personal benefits. For individuals, teams, and whole organizations, the capacity to constructively navigate disagreements and negotiate mutually agreeable solutions is tremendously valuable. Some of the rewards that come with learning these vital life skills include:

Stronger relationships result from collaboratively handling difficulties respectfully through open communication and compromise. People who can settle conflicts calmly and empathetically gain trust and see improvements in social bonds at work and home over time. This leads to greater productivity, as cooperation replaces distress and resentment between colleagues or family members.

Mental well-being benefits from avoiding the destructive cycle of stress, discord, and withdrawal that poor management can spark. Resolving issues constructively provides closure that alleviates lingering tensions, helping people feel in control of their circumstances. This boosts mood, self-esteem, and overall life satisfaction. The ability to navigate disputes smoothly facilitates more fulfillment across spheres of life.

Meanwhile, businesses realize gains like higher employee retention and morale for those cultivating a culture of mediation over aggression or avoidance when problems emerge. Workers are happier and healthier in harmonious environments, resulting in increased creativity, dedication, and output. Customers also tend to favor organizations with reputations for fairness, remaining loyal as a result.

Strong mediation expertise likewise proves to be an invaluable career asset. Resume opportunities abound for those capable of ushering colleagues, teams, or clients through trying periods to successful outcomes. Conflict specialists are in high demand across many industries for their ability to keep even huge, complex projects on track. These in-demand professionals experience fulfillment, serving as peacemakers and receiving financial rewards from such capabilities.

Overall, developing conflict management prowess provides a long list of returns through happier relationships, increased well-being, productive resolutions, and career growth. These proficiencies prove worth continual refinement as a priority life skill for personal achievement and making positive impacts in communities at large through cooperation instead of discord.

CHAPTER 13

EMPATHY IN LEADERSHIP

"Empathy is the bridge between two hearts, allowing us to connect, understand, and support each other even in the silence of unspoken emotions."

- Anonymous

While competence and vision are certainly important leadership qualities, the ability to understand people's perspectives and connect on an emotional level has perhaps never been more valuable in today's complex world. There appears to be a problematic disconnect between many who have risen to positions of power and authority and the lived experiences of those they govern or oversee. An alarmingly common failure to empathize with how policies and management decisions impact real people's lives threatens to undermine trust and progress.

This lack of empathy in leadership seems to be reflected across various sectors of society. In government, for example, there are charges that some policymakers have become detached from constituents and communities affected by their decisions, sometimes pursuing ideological agendas over practical needs. Likewise, in corporations, annual reports emphasize figures over humanity, potentially at the expense of worker well-being, customer relations, and greater social impacts. Even non-profits and charities have been accused of bureaucratization that loses touch with those they aim to serve.

The consequences can include unrest, low morale, high turnover, and other symptoms of disconnected workplaces or governed populations that feel powerlessness and lack of voice. Empathy is a two-way street; leaders must consider how their words and actions land and listen keenly to understand perspectives outside their own position and experience. Without this, plans and visions risk failing due to not being grounded in the human realities they touch.

Critics argue prevailing leadership models overly emphasize dominance and control while slighting softer relationship skills. Yet current global challenges like pandemics, conflicts, and climate issues demand nothing less than bringing people together around shared hopes. Leaders will fall short if they lack the caring, compassion, and wisdom to meaningfully relate with citizens and employees on deep human levels, which inspires true commitment to difficult tasks.

While some positions necessarily rely more on authority, even the most commanding roles can benefit from infusing decisions with an understanding of diverse end-users and stakeholders. Leaders in every sphere would do well at internalizing others' viewpoints and reconnecting business, policies, and initiatives to their ultimate purpose of improving lives, communities, and societies at large. With mounting calls for renewed empathy, those hoping to guide others would be wise to walk in varied shoes before asking others to follow their lead.

The Importance of Empathy in Effective Leadership

To be an inspiring leader who motivates others to achieve ambitious goals requires more than stern directives; it demands a proficient understanding of people on emotional levels. Effective guidance connects grand visions with very real human experiences through empathy, care, and compassion. Leaders lacking this vital quality will struggle to harness collective abilities toward shared purposes, regardless of technical aptitude or strategic acumen. Some key reasons empathy defines outstanding leadership include:

Relatability and retention are perhaps the most important outcomes of truly empathetic leadership. When people feel understood by those in charge, it dramatically changes the dynamics of any organization or group. Empathy is the bridge that connects vision with day-to-day reality by acknowledging shared experiences on a human level.

A leader who can empathize with the challenges facing employees, customers, or citizens earns instant trust. By demonstrating active listening and seeking first to understand diverse viewpoints, they break down barriers that often divide management from frontline staff. Showing care and concern for others' wellbeing, not just productivity or results, makes even difficult guidance feel supportive rather than dictatorial.

This authentic connection, cultivated through empathy, cultivates rapport and goodwill as a leader's foremost assets. It signals that those in charge will handle issues compassionately rather than punitively if problems do arise. Over time, that assurance nourishes a workplace culture where people freely contribute their best work and ideas without fear of unfair consequences.

However, perhaps empathy's greatest impact is on retention and morale. When workers feel respected for who they are in addition to what they produce, they reciprocate with unparalleled dedication to the overall mission. People will endure countless hardships if they believe their leader empathizes with the struggle and has their back unconditionally. That sense of solidarity alleviates so much workplace stress, discord, and medical costs associated with burnout.

More than any policy, empathy at its core keeps talent committed for the long run. Knowing their well-being matters provides intrinsic rewards, offsetting any dissatisfaction with external factors like pay and benefits. This, in turn, stabilizes operations by reducing expensive turnover while fostering consistency, productivity, and collaboration above all else.

In summary, true empathy elevates leadership beyond tactical skills by transforming the human dynamic that defines any shared purpose. It lays the relational foundation wherein people naturally motivate each other to excel through solidarity instead of scarcity. That cooperative spirit born of understanding is the most meaningful asset any group can possess.

Productivity increases in caring, psychologically safe climates where mistakes incur learning, not punishment. Empathy's attentive, nonjudgmental nature draws out members' fullest potential by promoting experimentation without fear of reprisal. This unleashes previously untapped facets of talent and intelligence toward shared ends.

Insight multiplies as empathetic concern primes open feedback channels, augmenting leaders' perspectives. Discerning how proposals affect varied stakeholders broadens consideration of perspectives leaders may have overlooked. Empathy cultivates two-way understanding, deepening appreciation of systemic complexities.

Resilience strengthens under empathetic guidance cognizant of humanity's shared fragilities. Compassion equips organizations to navigate difficulties with calm, wise adaptation instead of volatile reactionism. It engenders perseverance through understanding that nobody remains immune to hardships or doubt.

While commanding can inspire in moments, true leadership transforms lives. Empathy provides the nurturing conditions wherein every member may blossom for enduring change. It links overarching visions with on-the-ground realities through care, elevating both individuals and collectives to hitherto unimagined achievements.

How Empathy Strengthens Organizational Leadership

While qualities like strategy and vision are indispensable for guiding a company or non-profit, empathetic leadership substantially boosts effectiveness, productivity, and outcomes. Recent social science research strongly indicates that the ability to understand employees' lived experiences and connect with them on an emotional level creates significant benefits at both individual and systemic levels within an organization. Some ways an empathetic approach improves leadership include:

Staff retention is much higher when people feel truly valued beyond their output. Empathetic leaders who listen with compassion to professional and personal challenges engender loyalty through difficult periods. This stable workforce saves on recruitment and training costs and ensures smooth operations as relationships and institutional knowledge grow over time.

Productivity lifts as empathy fosters an environment where people feel inspired to go above and beyond rather than resentfully meeting minimum quotas. Autonomy, experimentation, and teamwork flourish without fear of judgment for mistakes made in pursuit of excellence. This unlocks discretionary effort and untapped talents that drive breakthroughs.

Innovation accelerates with empathetic leaders adept at understanding diverse stakeholder perspectives within and outside the organization. They apply diverse viewpoints to envision impactful solutions that others may overlook. This expands the organization's perspective and resourcefulness to tackle complex problems from new angles.

Decision-making improves through empathetic consultations, wherein followers feel safe sharing candidly without reprisal. Leaders gain insight into how proposals affect varied constituencies, spotlighting impacts to mitigate. This collaborative process cultivates buy-in, resilience, and high-quality outcomes attuned to reality.

Financial performance tends to exceed expectations at organizations led with empathy and care for people as much as profits. Studies link this "conscious capitalism" approach to reduced costs, greater customer/investor loyalty, and sustained growth over time through engaged, committed workforces innovating changes that elevate lives.

Overall, an empathetic leadership style that transforms a company into a nurturing community creates significant competitive advantages that no policy or procedure alone can match. Caring leaders inspire the best in every individual and team, driving the achievement of a shared noble purpose.

Empathetic Leadership in Action

While the benefits of empathy in leadership are well documented, seeing real-world examples provides powerful inspiration. Recent history has given us glimpses of leaders who understood the profound impact of caring, compassion, and genuine understanding on mobilizing collective achievement.

Nelson Mandela's guidance in post-Apartheid South Africa exemplified empathetic statesmanship. Efforts to dismantle systems of oppression and unite diverse populations demanded delicacy and moral vision. As a leader who endured hardship himself, Mandela grasped constituencies' varied plights and hard-won trust through displays of empathy, magnanimity, and grace during turbulent change. His conciliatory approach has been credited with averting bloodshed and setting Southern Africa on a path of reconciliation.

On a corporate level, visionaries like Starbucks' Howard Schultz demonstrated empathy, elevating entire industries. Schultz grasped employees' desire for fair compensation and benefits amid economic insecurity. The Starbucks "conscious capitalism" model stimulated loyalty and innovation by prioritizing worker wellness, driving global success. Similarly, consider Toyota's preeminent success in nurturing "respect for people" from the factory floor up.

Non-profit pioneers like Muhammad Yunus exemplified empathy, translating vision into large-scale impact. Observing impoverished communities' unmet needs, Yunus developed microcredit strategies empowering women. Grasping social complexities, he positioned his innovations as drivers of widespread development. On a local scale, compassion catalyzes community-based problem-solving worldwide through organizations like food banks, hospices, and literacy programs.

While specific contexts differ, common threads unite these exemplars: empathy facilitates grasps of constituents' full humanity beyond surface demographics; care understands challenges from others' shoes; and compassion elevates societies by cultivating each person's potential. Their examples remind us that leadership entails more than directives; it requires appreciating how visions affect diverse lives and harnessing collective strengths through empathy's capacity to uplift and unite.

CHAPTER 14

EMOTIONAL INTELLIGENCE IN RELATIONSHIPS

"The true strength of a relationship lies in our ability to manage our emotions, understand the needs of others and communicate with love and respect, even when it's difficult."
                                                        -Dr. Kimberly Pinckney

Building strong, lasting bonds with others requires much more than intellect; it is significantly shaped by one's emotional awareness and skills. The ability to recognize and manage feelings, both our own and others, forms the core of what is called emotional intelligence. It determines the quality of our interactions and attachments more than any other single factor. Some ways emotional intelligence defines relationships include:

Empathy is key to understanding perspectives different from our own. Without grasping emotions beneath surface words and actions, it is easy for misunderstandings to develop and distance to grow between people over time. Emotional intelligence helps "walk in another's shoes" through attentive listening with compassion.

Self-awareness of reactions and triggers allows for appropriately expressing needs and setting boundaries while regulating instinctive responses that could damage bonds or destroy intimacy through hurtful speech. Catching feelings before they escalate disputes models regulation for partners as well.

Social adroitness prevents isolation through the perceptiveness of social cues and cultural norms guiding smooth interactions. It facilitates repair when offenses occur by discerning intentions from impacts and resolving conflicts constructively before wounds fester. Teams flourish with emotional intelligence support.

Managing stress maintains calm, rational thinking when pressures rise and prevents lashing out at loved ones. Diffusing tensions protects relationships from cracking under duress while building resilience against future hardship through unified problem-solving.

Emotional expression strengthens intimacy by honestly yet considerately sharing inner experiences, thoughts, and vulnerabilities to cultivate emotional transparency, understanding, and closeness. This breeds trust, which is central to healthy relationships.

While factors like shared interests, values, and vision cement partnerships intellectually, emotional competence nurtures psychological safety and care, where bonds can thrive for lifetimes as circumstances change. This invisible glue is vital for translating affinity into enduring attachment throughout life.

The Strains of Low Emotional Intelligence in Relationships

While intellectual and physical attributes hold value, emotional competence plays perhaps the greatest role in sustaining long-term intimate bonds. Failures of self-awareness, empathy, or regulation inevitably damage close partnerships if left unaddressed. Some issues that often arise include:

Misunderstandings are frequent without the perspective-taking to grasp another's viewpoint or the social skills to navigate sensitivities. As intimacy recedes, this breeds frustration, disengagement, and silent treatment between couples.

Resentment builds when one cannot express needs considerately while triggering conflict through criticism instead of an "I statement" regulating reactivity. Over time, this taxes the perception of care and respect in the relationship.

Trust erodes without the vulnerability of personal disclosure or the ability to resolve disputes constructively through compromise. Partners may withdraw intimacy as resentment or bitterness simmers beneath avoidant behaviors.

Codependency strains the dynamic where one lacks independence but smothers the other without boundaries. Or influences controlling behaviors by trying to suppress raw emotions that threaten stability. *Both damage equity.*

Stress on mental health escalates without outlets like regulating distress through self-care, empathy for a partner's bad days, or teamwork in navigating hard times as a united front. This taxes well-being.

Commitment wavers under accumulated discontentment rather than addressing its emotional roots jointly through patience, active listening without defensiveness, and willingness to grow together.

While no couple agrees on everything, low emotional intelligence multiplies dissonance, which is too great for many bonds to withstand gracefully. Committing to developing these skills strengthens understanding and preserves what partners cherish most.

Cultivating Emotional Intelligence for Stronger Bonds

While deficits in emotional skills often strain relationships over time, cultivating key competencies provides potent tools for building understanding, trust, and psychological safety between partners. Some strategies couples report benefiting from include:

Deep listening through attentive focus without distraction helps each person feel heard fully without interruption. Asking gentle clarifying questions prevents assumptions, while reflective paraphrasing conveys attempts to grasp another's perspective accurately and with care.

Validating feelings by acknowledging the emotion's sense rather than dismissing it, even if behavior warrants discussion, fosters dignity and openness in sharing vulnerabilities. This separates events from identities to foster intimacy.

Compromising respectfully when views differ by finding common ground and valuing mutual needs equally helps tensions dissolve into cooperation, seeking synergistic third options. Flexibility lubricates teamwork.

Resolving conflicts productively rather than avoidance, hostility, or withdrawal keeps rifts from festering beneath surface calm. Addressing the inherent dignity of disagreements promotes long-term healing.

Expressing gratitude, not just grievances, through honest yet considerate affirmations of what one admires in one partner cultivates positivity when frustrations could dominate. Managing stress adaptively and autonomously through outlets like mindfulness, exercise, and rest relieves tensions that sabotage even strong relationships under duress without release valves.

Commitment to growth as individuals and as a team through education and applying new understanding with patience helps redress old detrimental patterns and reinvent bonds to survive challenges.

Prioritizing time for fun, intimacy, and shared interests amidst busyness renews foundations beneath superficial ups and downs. Flexibility lubricates teamwork. Adapting these strategies likely transforms relationships from rote to rewarding through empathy, cooperation, and renewed connection, replacing potential discord. Continued dedication preserves sanctuaries of care.

Building Strong Bonds Through Emotional Intelligence

Cultivating awareness and management of emotions holds myriad benefits for fostering intimate, satisfying relationships. A few key advantages of developing emotional intelligence include

Deeper Understanding

One of the most valuable aspects of emotional intelligence is the capacity for deep empathy—to not just hear what a partner is saying but to truly grasp how they feel and why. This awareness of underlying emotions is foundational for building intimacy as well as navigating life's hardships within a relationship. When challenges arise, the ability to understand another's perspective makes all the difference.

Rather than instinctively becoming defensive or detached, developing empathy allows for remaining open and attentive even during tensions. By perceiving the unspoken feelings shaping a view, defusing potential conflicts or repairing misunderstandings becomes much more achievable. It signifies an effort to walk in another's shoes with care and non-judgment.

This nurtures a sense that one is not alone in facing difficulties, sparing rifts from forming during periods that could otherwise pull people apart.

Being emotionally attuned to this level also facilitates honest discussions that strengthen long-term relational bonds. It prompts the comprehensive observation of issues from all angles to find cooperative solutions that respect all parties, versus adversarial stances that risk win-lose outcomes. Approaching problems empathetically communicates the desire to sustain the well-being of both individuals and the relationship as a whole.

Perhaps most significantly, empathy provides sanctuary for vulnerabilities during distress. It conveys unconditional acceptance of a partner's humanity, experiences, and emotions rather than pressuring repression or minimizing struggles. Feeling truly understood without fear of reprisal or stigma nurtures resilience, enabling couples to survive hardships that defeat many others.

Overall, the ability to grasp another's perspective forms an emotionally safe space where intimacy and trust may flourish throughout life's ups and downs. It transforms potentially fracturing circumstances into opportunities, strengthening compassion and partnership through shared tribulations.

Healthier Communication

One of the most impactful skills in any close relationship is communicating effectively, especially during disagreements or challenging periods. Practicing mindful awareness of one's reactions and employing empathetic listening plays a major role here. Proper expression and attention foster understanding instead of potential discord.

Regulating instinctive impulses through deep breathing or removing oneself from an emotional moment if needed allows one to eventually speak with care, versus potentially saying things regretted later in heated passion. Conveying personal feelings and needs using "I statements" like "I feel X when Y happens" prevents blaming tones that induce defensiveness from a partner.

This regulates tensions while still enabling the surface of needs. It takes effort, but it cultivates a cooperative dynamic through fairness and accountability. In turn, a partner feels safe to explain their perspective openly as well through reciprocal understanding.

Active listening is just as important as expressing oneself. Making eye contact, asking gentle questions, and paraphrasing what someone shared with them ensures comprehension beyond just hearing words. It conveys the full presence and validation of their emotions or situation. Partners feel heard and cared for instead of retreating into stubborn silence.

Together, these practices facilitate productive discussions, resolving issues respectfully, and strengthening intimacy beyond superficial resolutions. Even difficult topics addressed empathetically can promote healing and build greater trust in facing life's challenges as a united team. Prioritizing clear expression and patience with each other provides tools for maintaining healthy long-term bonds. There is no denying that communication holds the relationship together, so techniques to enhance it prove worthwhile.

Improved Conflict Resolution

Healthy relationships require navigating disagreements respectfully instead of avoidance or hostility that damages intimacy over time. One key strategy is cultivating the ability to find cooperative resolutions while valuing perspectives equally. This strengthens underlying trust far beyond any one conflict addressed.

Perspective-taking lies at the heart of collaborative problem-solving. Making a sincere effort to understand where one's partner is coming from, even if initially disagreeing, shows care for their well-being along with one's own needs. It frames issues as shared challenges to overcome together versus personal attacks. This opens minds and hearts towards compromise.

As it says, "You can't always control circumstances. However, you can always control your own thoughts."
— Charles Popplestone

Compromise doesn't mean settling or making full concessions; it means crafting solutions that are agreeable to all parties. It may involve brainstorming options, weighing pros and cons together, or finding novel alternatives while respecting multiple viewpoints. Synergistic resolutions uphold each person's dignity rather than winners and losers. Partners feel heard as a team working for mutual benefit.

Addressing difficulties constructively and with care reaffirms the bond's resilience through life's inevitable tensions. It conveys faith that any obstacle can be navigated without damaging closeness by prioritizing understanding and cooperation. Over time, this transforms disputes into opportunities to strengthen interdependence and trust that persists beyond surface-level issues.

With practice, cooperative conflict resolution becomes second nature within the relationship. It serves as a sanctuary, weathering challenges that defeat many other partnerships. Overall, prioritizing empathetic problem-solving lays the groundwork for intimate bonds built to withstand life's tests, large and small.

Increased Intimacy

At the core of any deeply fulfilling relationship is the capacity for true emotional intimacy—the ability to openly share one's inner thoughts and feelings without fear of judgment or rejection. Cultivating authentic emotional connection is largely built upon fostering a sense that one feels truly understood by one's partner.

Feeling emotionally "seen" provides profound reassurance that it is safe to be vulnerable. It conveys unconditional acceptance of another's humanity in all its complexity, beyond just smiles and achievements. Partners understand that behind superficial expressions lies a deeper inner landscape that constantly evolves.

This degree of trust and care encourages disclosing private hopes, fears, and inner workings of the mind or heart that define individual experience. Sharing these inner depths transforms individuals from strangers to soulmates intimately intertwined on a psychological level, matching or surpassing physical closeness.

Over time, deepening self-awareness and emotional literacy leads to more fulfilling insights into life and each other through disclosure. Bonds grow profoundly meaningful on an authentic level, versus superficial companionship alone. Partners feel centered in their relationship through the acceptance of inner truth.

While it is scary to reveal vulnerabilities, emotional intimacy paradoxically fosters greater strength, agency, and independence within the relationship. Each feels empowered to weather challenges with unflinching support. Authenticity becomes liberating versus confinement or pretension that damages bonds.

To conclude, being grounded in fully grasping another's internal experience elevates partnerships that endure life's uncertainties. This psychological and emotional closeness brings joy that shallow interactions alone could never impart for as long as hearts shall live.

Enhanced Cooperation

Building strong relationships requires navigating life's ever-changing landscape together smoothly as a cohesive unit. Cultivating social and cultural adaptability through emotional intelligence plays a vital role here. It broadens partners' perspectives on situations while strengthening their ability to face challenges seamlessly as a team.

Socio-emotional skills like empathy, self-awareness, and regulation facilitate the perceptiveness of implicit norms and expectations within various environments, communities, or family dynamics. This helps couples understand their surroundings and navigate them fluidly without friction. Partners intuitively grasp how to address cultural differences and sensitively honor each other's backgrounds.

Such flexibility also lubricates collaboration alongside differing personalities, temperaments, love languages, and problem-solving styles within the relationship itself. Rather than rigidly insisting on one approach alone as superior, embracing diversities allows for weaving strengths into synergies. Compromise comes organically from valuing various viewpoints.

Perhaps most significantly, socio-emotional adroitness provides invaluable tools for weathering inevitable life changes together. It cultivates resilience against upheavals like career shifts, relocations far from familiar support systems, aging parents requiring more support, or other unexpected challenges altering dynamics. Partners experience solid adaptation, minimizing disruptions.

Cultivating social and emotional fluidity enhances any bond's ability to handle complexities smoothly through understanding diverse perspectives. It broadens horizons against potential insularity while strengthening collaboration, which is indispensable for navigating life's unpredictable difficulties side by side. Flexibility forms the basis of partnerships capable of flourishing through all stages.

Stronger Commitment

At the core of any lasting relationship lies a profound awareness of our shared human experience—that beneath surface variances in opinions, backgrounds, or temperaments, all people experience the same spectrum of emotion. Cultivating empathy for a partner's joys and struggles reinforces this profound connection essential for resilience.

Taking time to comprehend another's feelings, even when joyful events may elicit envy or difficulties stir frustration, preserves intimacy. It conveys compassion for their inherent dignity and happiness, despite the inevitable differences in how life unfolds for each. Partners recognize that life's beauty and hardships unite far more than any superficiality could divide.

This perspective transmutes difficulties from threats to the bond into opportunities that cement care. Being present through challenging periods, not just celebrating wins together, builds unshakeable trust in mutual support through uncertainty. Empathy strengthens interdependence rather than distancing itself under stress, strengthening resilience for whatever lies ahead.

Small, thoughtful gestures reflecting awareness of a loved one's inner experience can lift spirits immensely. Preparing a favorite meal during sadness or sending heartfelt wishes amidst exciting news nurtures fulfillment beyond surface-level interactions alone. It affirms the profound significance of being seen, heard, and cared for as part of the essence of being.

Overall, consciously appreciating our common humanity above all temporarily separates but ultimately unites and provides an emotional sanctuary, nourishing any relationship's capacity to not just endure but thrive despite obstacles that defeat less cognizant pairs. Empathy transforms challenges into the privilege of experiencing life's range together.

Greater Well-being

"When we are no longer able to change a situation, we are challenged to change ourselves."

— Viktor Frank

A strong relationship requires prioritizing both individual health and the bond's stability equally. Partners must fulfill personal needs, care for each other, and attend to duties. Emotional intelligence plays a key supportive role here through promoting balanced mental fitness—the basis of any intimate connection's prosperity.

Healthy outlets prove indispensable for alleviating daily stresses from work, family, or other responsibilities that deplete health if untreated. Activities like exercise, art, meditation, or quality time with friends provide sanctuary while sustaining personal passions significant to the agency. This nurtures strength, returning bountifully to relationships.

In tandem, independence amid interdependence prevails when partners respect boundaries, protecting individualism. However, codependence threatens festering resentments when one's needs go chronically unmet despite voicing them. Autonomy balanced with teamwork keeps spillover stresses from corroding closeness.

Self-awareness regarding emotions and limits, then effective communication, must navigate them respectfully and sustain equilibrium. Compromise satisfies the requirements of oneself and others reasonably to prevent affairs of daily living from dictating long-term well-being or partnership functioning.

It is important to prioritize mental fitness to safeguard bonds from potential damage wrought by unaddressed wounds, tensions, or imbalances that fester below surface tranquility over time. It nourishes a partnership's resilience and each person's ability to freely bring their full humanity and joy to its domain. Wellness supplies love's most fertile soil. Emotional intelligence cultivates relational skills, transforming fleeting attractions into profound lifelong friendships through understanding, trust, and care rather than surface attributes alone. Its benefits compound greatly over the years, navigating life's difficulties together.

CHAPTER 15

EMOTIONAL SAFETY AND IT'S SIGNIFICANCE

"Emotional safety is the foundation of trust and openness; without it, relationships wither, but with it, they flourish into spaces where vulnerability is celebrated and growth is nurtured."

-Anonymous

Emotional safety is a sense of trust that allows us to openly share our feelings without fear of judgment or retaliation. It's the confidence that being vulnerable will not damage a relationship but strengthen understanding between people who care for one another. Where emotional safety exists, honest conversation and self-expression thrive. Partners feel heard and accepted for who they are inside. Both parties know they won't be attacked, minimized, or defined by the emotions they bring to light - even difficult ones.

This freedom from threat fosters intimacy. Rather than hiding parts of ourselves, we can let our emotional guards down and truly connect on a deep level. Our authentic selves are not only accepted but cherished as well. Emotional safety is a critical component of secure attachment between human beings. From an early age, it teaches us that opening our hearts will lead to nurturing bonds, not harm. This directly shapes our ability to manage feelings in all kinds of relationships throughout life.

When emotional safety is consistent, trust is built over time. Loved ones feel confident relying on each other, communicating needs, and supporting one another through both joy and struggle. They've learned to tap into empathy, forgiveness, and understanding even during disputes. Emotions require practice to navigate well. Environments where expressing all feelings meets acceptance provide a laboratory to build this skill. The security allows for honesty even if mistakes happen - strengthening the capacity for emotional intelligence.

Overall, prioritizing emotional safety sets the tone for healthy interactions, which are defined by care, comfort, and respect between people. It cultivates resilience within, empowering individuals to remain true to themselves while also considering others with compassion. Relationships thrive on this foundation.

Building Emotional Safety

Communication: Open communication helps build trust and emotional safety. Listening actively by making eye contact, asking questions, and paraphrasing is important to fully understand others' perspectives. Validating feelings, instead of advice-giving, leaves room for true empathy.

Trust: Honesty must also be balanced with compassion. If trust or boundaries are broken, acknowledge the impact but focus on rebuilding positively through transparent discussion of needs and boundaries and how to meet them moving forward.

Boundaries: Set firm but fair personal boundaries to avoid confusion. Clearly defining limits upfront lets relationships develop healthily within established comfort levels for all parties. Boundaries must be respected to feel secure sharing vulnerability.

Vulnerability: Some vulnerability is necessary for closeness, yet sharing deeply personal information risks pain. Manage this risk by establishing trust and ensuring the environment respects emotional well-being. Not every confidence needs to be reciprocated to demonstrate care and acceptance of another's humanity.

Supportive Environment: It may take effort after experiences leaving one gun-shy, but slowly opening up strengthens connections. Shared joy, frustrations, and failures bond individuals closer as equals - though authentic relationships embrace all unvarnished parts of a person without demands.

Most importantly, cultivate a space where all voices feel heard, none are attacked, and empathy reigns over blame. Prioritize understanding each other as complex individuals deserving dignity. Discuss problems respectfully to find cooperative solutions honoring everyone's needs and humanity. Here, emotional safety can thrive.

Challenges to Emotional Safety

Recognizing Unsafe Situations

Pay attention to behavior that disrespects boundaries, like excessive pressure, manipulation, or isolation from others.

Take any threats, belittling, humiliation, or harsh criticisms from partners seriously.

Note tendencies to dismiss or invalidate your experiences and feelings on a regular basis.

Conflict Resolution

Express how certain issues make you feel calmly and actively listen to understand others' perspectives without judgment.

Compromise when possible by finding shared interests or areas where both sides can gain.

Seek mediation from an impartial party if tensions remain high during discussions.

Self-Care

Take occasional breaks from an emotionally taxing relationship by spending time with other loved ones.

Engage in activities you find relaxing and meaningful to process stressful experiences.

Make sure your basic needs are met so you enter conflicts from a place of empowerment rather than reactivity.

Practical Exercises

Reflect through journaling on interactions that strengthen versus threaten your emotional safety. Note behaviors to preserve or boundaries to establish going forward.

With a partner, you trust role-play scenarios where boundaries are respected after being communicatively set in a caring manner. Practice calming techniques like deep breathing if tensions arise, too.

Dealing with Narcissism and Intimate Partner Abuse

Narcissism is an excessive admiration of oneself and a lack of empathy for others. Narcissists often have an inflated sense of their own importance and entitlement. They often take advantage of or exploit others to reach their own goals or boost their ego.

Intimate partner abuse refers to harmful behaviors used to gain power and control over a partner in an intimate relationship, such as marriage or dating. It can include emotional, physical, or sexual violence. Abusive partners often isolate their victims from others, threaten them, or hurt them physically to assert dominance.

Emotional intelligence is the ability to understand and manage our own emotions and recognize emotions in others. It involves skills like self-awareness, self-regulation, motivation, empathy, and social skills. People with high emotional intelligence tend to handle relationships and conflicts in a healthier way.

Understanding Narcissism

Narcissism is characterized by an inflated sense of self-importance and lack of empathy. Individuals with narcissistic traits often believe they are special or unique and require constant admiration from others. In relationships, this ego and entitlement can manifest in an overwhelming need to be the center of attention and insensitivity to a partner's feelings. Narcissists also tend to believe they are superior to others and can become jealous or critical if their partner receives any praise or recognition.

The dynamics of narcissistic abuse deserve examination to better understand the detrimental impacts. Individuals who abuse this way seek to control their partner by imposing their will and opinions as law. In the early stages of a relationship, an abusive partner may shower the victim with affection and attention in a process known as "idealization." This makes the victim feel cared for and leaves them vulnerable once the devaluing phase starts. Gradually, small criticisms or put-downs undermine the victim's self-esteem and independence. Isolation from friends and family commonly occurs to allow the abuser maximum dominance.

If a victim starts resisting demands or asserting their own needs, the abuser often switches to emotional attacks, threats, gaslighting, or other manipulative behaviors aimed at regaining power. This idealize-devalue cycle chips away at the partner's sense of worth and reality. Eventually, some relationships reach a "discard" phase involving the abuser withdrawing care and leaving the victim confused and hurt. Without understanding the psychological roots, it's easy for victims to feel responsible for the changing attitudes when, in fact, the abuse stems from their partner's disordered needs. Greater public awareness can help recognize these damaging dynamics earlier to prevent harm.

Impact of Narcissism on Emotional Well-Being

Manipulation is a powerful tool that narcissists use to exercise control over their partners. Because they lack empathy, narcissists do not see their victims as fully human--only as objects that exist to serve their grandiose sense of self. This allows them to disregard a partner's feelings and manipulate them purely for selfish gains.

Some common manipulation tactics include ignoring a partner's boundaries, trivializing their concerns, and changing the subject to re-center discussions around themselves. Isolation is also frequently used to limit outside social ties that could offer an alternative viewpoint. Over time, these behaviors chip away at self-esteem until the partner feels they cannot do anything right.

A related insidious tactic is gaslighting. This occurs when someone denies events, conversations, or behaviors that actually happened and makes the other person question their own reality and judgment. Gaslighters will lie and then claim the victim is "too sensitive" or "misremembering" when confronted. This erodes the foundation of trust within a relationship. Some signs of gaslighting include a partner frequently contradicting your accounts of incidents, blaming you for things they did, or minimizing their abusive actions.

Being in a relationship with a narcissist can take a large psychological toll, leaving people depressed, anxious, and uncertain of themselves. Constant criticism, invalidation of boundaries, and gaslighting warp one's sense of self over months or years. It is a form of prolonged emotional abuse that is difficult to recognize from within due to its subtle and insidious nature. Greater societal empathy is needed for those recovering from narcissistic abuse and rebuilding confidence in their own perceptions.

Intimate Partner Abuse

Relationships are meant to be nurturing and bring out the best in one another, but sadly, this is not always the case. When one person exerts power and control over their partner through threats, insults, or actions meant to demean them, it is considered abuse. Abuse comes in various forms, and the effects can be damaging if left unaddressed.

Emotional abuse is perhaps one of the more subtle yet impactful types. Through constant criticism, mind games, isolation from friends and family, or threats to end the relationship, the victim's sense of self is chipped away until they doubt their own judgments. Over time, this type of abuse can really shake someone's confidence and make it difficult to trust their own perceptions. Psychological abuse involves intentionally saying or doing things to scare, intimidate, or control a person. Tactics like yelling, smashing things, or threatening violence aim to coerce the victim into submitting to the abuser's will through fear.

Physical violence leaves marks, but financial abuse also deprives a person of independence. Withholding money, spending excessively, or prohibiting the other partner from working hinders their ability to support themselves if the need arises. The abuser maintains power, and the victim becomes reliant on the whims of the other. All these behaviors are meant to undermine someone and erode their sense of agency, which is why abuse is never strictly a private matter between two people.

The insidious nature of abuse makes its effects hard to recognize at first. Over the long run, however, studies show intimate partner violence takes a serious toll on mental well-being. Survivors are more likely to develop anxiety, depression, or post-traumatic stress disorder as they relive past trauma through intrusive thoughts and flashbacks. Trust issues often linger, making it challenging for them to feel safe or commit to future relationships even years after leaving the abuser. The prolonged stress also has physical impacts like disrupted sleep cycles and higher risks for chronic health conditions.

Abuse profoundly changes how someone views themselves and perceives normal interactions. Constantly being put down or controlled undermines self-esteem, making people doubt their capabilities. Over time, the victim may normalize abusive behaviors as they lose sight of what is considered acceptable treatment within relationships. Forming new bonds afterward proves difficult when someone lacks the confidence to maintain healthy communication and set boundaries with partners. Relationships are about support, care, and mutual respect. Sadly, abuse prevents people from experiencing care freely in a way that nourishes both individuals.

There is hope, though, as with time and support, survivors of abuse can regain a stronger sense of self and learn to trust their inner strength once more. Therapy helps process trauma, while support groups provide a safe community for shared experiences. Friends and loved ones play a huge role in showing care, patience, and acceptance as someone rebuilds. With continued positive influences and self-care practices, healing is definitely possible. Ultimately, talking honestly about these issues helps dispel stigma so people feel empowered to get help and know their worth isn't defined by the actions of others.

Strategies for Dealing with Narcissism and Abuse

Learning to set boundaries is critically important for one's well-being and health. In unhealthy relationships where a partner exhibits narcissistic, selfish behaviors by ignoring your feelings and putting their own needs first at your expense, clear limits must be defined to prevent harm. But doing so requires believing you deserve respect and realizing acceptable standards exist for how you allow others to treat you.

The first step involves honest self-reflection on needs, values, and areas that cause discomfort when crossed. It's normal to please others. However, true happiness comes from caring for yourself, too. Don't be afraid to voice how actions affect you, whether positive or negative, using calm statements pairing "I feel" with the reason. Stand up for your right to say no without excuse or apology. Initially, the narcissist may react poorly to restricted control, but firm consistency over time is necessary.

Self-care is vital when dealing with difficult people, as their actions say more about them than you. Spend relaxing alone time with trusted friends who build you up, pursue hobbies nourishing your mind/body, and seek counseling if feelings overwhelm you. Addressing stress through healthy outlets tempers reactions and permits keeping perspective despite others' provocations intended to destabilize. A supportive outlet provides perspective to recognize manipulation techniques employed.

Should attempts to establish boundaries fail, leaving safely might become necessary rather than continuing damage. Know this doesn't equate to failure on your part; ending is sometimes the bravest choice. Communicate readiness calmly after making alternative living/financial plans in secret, which the narcissist cannot access. Stay contact-free afterward due to toxicity from accusatory messages meant to regain power over you.

In the aftermath of the ending, self-care remains paramount while processing mixed emotions. Time allowing wounds and trust to mend requires patience. Suppressing feelings by diving into activities delays true healing; addressing pain through talk therapy or survivor support groups with sympathizers uplifts spirits more directly. Self-reflection reveals confusing times, and clarity comes through accepting without judgment.

With assistance, look inward honestly and emerge stronger understanding traits, making others' approval seem integral while discovering your own wonderful qualities. Rediscover independence without defining value by now absent praise or threats seeking to degrade. Building self-worth from within outwardly over time strengthens against future toxicity's lure since being manipulated feels comfortable compared to unknowns of autonomy.

Trauma bonds form from intermittent reinforcement narcissists use, so remind yourself daily their actions resulted from personal deficiencies, not deficiencies within you deserved repairing mistreatment. Keep journaling, appreciate small joys, and nurture relationships that enhance life rather than focusing on past wrongs. Transforming self-talk uplifts mood, affecting interpretations gradually with practice. Overall, healing proves non-linear, yet it ultimately leads toward fuller days ahead built upon secure foundations within.

Resources and Support

Our ability to understand and navigate relationships skillfully requires achieving balance within ourselves first. We all experience life's ups and downs, yet those dealing with trauma face greater challenges in self-regulating emotions in healthy ways without triggering reminders of past pain. Learning mindfulness techniques like journaling feelings instead of bottling them up or talking through troubling thoughts with understanding listeners assists in processing distressing experiences over time. Taking measured steps at your pace respects personal healing limits.

While self-care remains important, preventing harm is also aided by learning to spot questionable behavior in others. Narcissism traits like constantly dismissing your views, isolating yourself from others, or finding fault in harmless actions aim to chip away at confidence until depending on the abuser seems safer than independence. Realizing how disrespect distorts a relationship allows defending personal boundaries with care, not reaction. Still, not all questionable relationships involve intentional abuse - many stem from mutual growth areas partners could address constructively through calm discussions where each feels heard without judgment.

With understanding comes compassion, even for those struggling to treat others kindly. Focusing on your health allows distancing from toxic influences while maintaining hope people can change with self-reflection and support. Meaningful bonds involve bringing out the best in one another through honest yet gentle discussions when discomfort arises instead of sweeping issues under the rug or attacking character during disagreements. Teamwork, not competition, is key.

Emotional intelligence growth helps navigate relationships safely by listening attentively to needs being expressed and responding constructively, not just with preferred solutions. Thoughts and feelings differ for all people based on varied experiences, so ask clarifying questions to ensure understanding before offering advice or opinions on sensitive topics to avoid unintended harm. Aim to resolve issues, not "win" disagreements at the other's expense, by focusing on shared long-term goals. These relationship skills bolster resiliently coping with complex emotions calmly, preventing lashing out or retreating during conflicts from past triggers.

Enhancing emotional awareness and competence benefits connections in a significant manner by promoting empathy, communication, and compromise. With patience and willingness to learn from mistakes, even past wounds may heal as fulfilling bonds form through mutual care, respect, and understanding between all people. While some partnerships cannot be salvaged, each growth experience acquired for applying refined skills adds purpose. Transitioning from just reacting emotionally aids in creating a safer world where people feel truly heard without judgment - the foundation for thriving relationships.

CHAPTER 16

NAVIGATING DIFFICULT CONVERSATIONS

"In the hardest conversations, emotional intelligence is our guide. It teaches us to listen deeply, speak kindly, and create an environment where understanding triumphs over the need to be right."

-Anonymous

Touching on sensitive subjects or deep confessions within a conversation can undoubtedly make the discussion more difficult and delicate to navigate. There are often very good reasons why some things are personal or private, as opening up fully always brings a risk of vulnerability or judgment from others. However, when trust is built between individuals, sharing at a deeper level can also lead to stronger bonds of understanding.

The key is knowing your audience and reading their cues to see how open they may be. Conversations are a two-way street, so listening as much as talking will provide insights into what the other person is comfortable with. Making assumptions or pressing for information someone is not ready to give can damage the relationship or cause hurt. At the same time, showing genuine care and interest in learning more about someone can help them feel safe to share at their own pace over time.

Taboo topics and private struggles often elicit challenging emotions in both the one disclosing and the listeners hearing about another's hardships. Having empathy, avoiding judgments, and responding with care, support, and wisdom can help people feel heard during difficult discussions.

However, others may need the space to choose how much they reveal for their own well-being. A balance is required between offering an open ear and respecting personal privacy.

Going off on emotional tangents or inserting one's unsolicited perspective too frequently can also steer conversations in an unfavorable direction. Maintaining focus on understanding the other individual instead of making everything about oneself results in improved dialogue. Allowing silences or changes in the subject when someone gets temporarily overwhelmed additionally grants them comfort and control within sensitive discussions.

Building trust little by little through a respectful exchange is key to opening up the potential for deeper sharing. But not forcing conversations into delicate territories before both parties feel at ease helps prevent relationship damage or trauma. With patience and empathy, meaningful discussions can help forge strong bonds and bring clarity and healing. However, sensitivity to each person's comfort level, as well as the circumstances, is always needed to ensure difficult talks ultimately benefit all involved. Communication works best through care, compassion, and consent between all participants.

The Challenges of Difficult Discussions

> "Between stimulus and response, there is a space. In that space is our power to choose our response. In our response lies our growth and our freedom."
>
> — Viktor Frankl

Many conversations that involve sensitive or personal matters tend to be sidestepped altogether due to how complicated they can become. Discussing subjects like politics, religion, trauma histories, or emotional vulnerabilities opens the door to the uncertainty that leaves people feeling unsafe. Easier topics that don't stir up difficult feelings are usually preferred instead.

When sensitivities are touched on, differing views are more likely to emerge, with hot buttons getting pressed. Disagreements can then escalate rather than resolve, as nuance gets lost amid defensiveness and hurt. No one wishes to engage in back-and-forths that devolve into hurtful exchanges without any gains being made. The possibility of conflict brewing causes instinctive avoidance to kick in to protect one's own comfort and limit potential drama.

Complex issues often do not neatly fit into easy answers either, leaving conversations without clear resolution. Ambiguity breeds more questions than solutions, as different life experiences shape how various topics are perceived. With so many perspectives to juggle and offend nobody, coming to an understanding gets tricky fast. The uncertainty fosters a desire to change the subject to something less polarizing that everyone can agree on peacefully.

Some people simply want to keep interactions lighthearted without analyzing problems deeply or hashing through disagreements too forcefully. Difficult talks demand high levels of attentive listening, processing of multiple viewpoints, and the ability to remain calm amid emotive topics— skills not everyone has in abundance. Staying in one's lane of lighter talks that flow nicely is sometimes the path of least resistance.

However, by circumventing challenging discussions, opportunities for connecting with and understanding others on a more meaningful level are also missed. With tact and patience, people of differing beliefs can find common ground or gain new perspectives on issues when they are willing to delve deeper. But opening Pandora's box also always entails risks, so most prefer keeping things simple and conflict-free if possible.

A balance must be found between avoidance of complexity for convenience's sake and facing issues head-on to enhance relationships. Some subjects will naturally prove too sensitive for many encounters, while others can be breached gradually with care, respect, and an open yet discerning mind.

If It's Difficult, Why Is It Important?

While tackling sensitive subjects or deepening discussions is inherently challenging work, the value it provides is significant. At their essence, conversations allow for a meeting of minds where perspectives outside one's own can be considered. Through exposing ourselves and others to new viewpoints in an atmosphere of respect, relationships are strengthened and understanding grows.

Awareness of differing life experiences and struggles is vastly expanded by sharing in depth. Walking in another's shoes and listening fully with empathy helps dissolve misconceptions over time. Dialogue moves us from mere coexistence to true community as bonds form across perceived divisions. Facing issues together bravely fosters the kind of societal progress that uplifts everyone.

"Knowing yourself is the beginning of all wisdom."
— Aristotle

Challenging talks permit delving into root causes rather than staying stuck on superficial levels or assumptions. Processing experiences together leads to useful insights, wisdom, and supportive problem-solving when comfort allows for candidness without judgment or reaction. Disagreements don't inherently damage closeness if handled respectfully through open communication.

Avoiding complexity prevents the opportunity for valuable insights and breakthroughs that shift perspectives toward the positive. Important problems persist when we don't join together thoughtfully in discussion. Silence ensures ignorance remains, while voices raised in truth and understanding can cut through it. Real intimacy and accord arise from a willingness to bear vulnerability to benefit the relationship.

For individuals, being heard deeply significantly aids growth, healing, and self-awareness. Fears diminish as misconceptions are clarified through dialogue with caring souls. Dark secrets lose power, and light is shed on new solutions when painful pasts find validation. Freely sharing inner truths bonds companions as closely as few other experiences can.

While discomfort inevitably arises within sensitive territory at times, facing it head-on through compassion yields far greater rewards than superficial comfort alone. Growth demands stretching beyond limitations, and conversations cutting to the core of who we are and what matters most clearly produce meaningful advancement. Together, by opening our minds and hearts, we build a society of deeper connection, care, and fulfillment for all.

Step-By-Step Guidance to Initiate

One of the most important things when broaching sensitive topics is establishing trust and openness from the beginning. Make it clear your goal is greater understanding, not argument. Listen fully without interruption to show care for the other person's perspective before sharing your own. Finding common ground, even if it is minor, can set a collaborative tone as well.

Asking thoughtful questions is preferable to making statements, as it avoids immediate defensiveness. Seek to learn someone's reasoning and heart behind a view, not just the surface view itself. Share personal experiences gently if it deepens the discussion productively. Check assumptions by rephrasing what you're hearing to confirm understanding, too.

Disagreements will likely arise, so controlling emotional reactions is key. Take pauses if needed and come from a place of calm rationale rather than reactions like frustration or contempt, which shut down dialogue. Finding middle perspectives and acknowledging valid parts of competing views can also smooth over tension and reveal potential new solutions.

Compromise and meeting halfway show respect, whereas winning arguments damage relationships. Difficult talks are marathons, not sprints; patience and pacing oneself allow sensitive sharing without overwhelming both sides. Changing topics or talking less seriously at times also maintains a safe vibe. Laughter together, where possible, enhances closeness.

Most importantly, remember that you're discussing ideas, not attacking characters. Keep the focus on issues, not people. If someone shuts down, accept them as they are for now, but the door stays open to revisit when you are comfortable. With care and understanding as ambitions, challenging conversations can strengthen what unites us far beyond any divide.

To understand it better, let's analyze a fictional scenario to understand the regulation of emotions and how navigation in difficult conversations helps us. Let's say there is growing tension between Abby and her friend or roommate, Ben. The rising expenses and lack of participation from Ben have been striking Abby's budget for some time. Of course, it's never easy to have a chat like this with a friend who's been around for a long time. Let's understand how Abby highlights the navigation strategies we mentioned above to dissolve their dispute.

Abby sighed as she entered the apartment, nerves bundling in her stomach. She and her roommate Ben had been dodging this talk for weeks but couldn't put it off any longer. Their living expenses had risen significantly with property taxes and utilities rising, yet Ben hadn't increased his share of costs.

As Abby began cooking dinner, Ben came home and plopped down to watch TV as usual. "Hey, how was your day?" Abby asked casually. "Oh, fine, you know. The usual," Ben replied without looking over. Abby bit her lip and said, "Actually, I was wondering if we could discuss something... not so usual."

Ben tensed, clicking off the TV reluctantly to face her. "Discuss what?" He asked blankly, hoping to skirt around details. But Abby knew they had to address the financial strain head-on to find a solution together. Gently, she explained how their costs had risen dramatically, yet his contributions hadn't changed at all, leaving her strapped.

"I'm not trying to make you feel bad," Abby assured. "Things happen beyond our control sometimes. I just want to figure this out together since we're in it as a team, you know?" Ben nodded hesitantly, but he couldn't meet her eyes. A frown emerged as he recalled how preoccupied he'd been with his own things lately.

Abby gave him space to think, focusing on cooking to avoid any confrontational vibes. After some beats of silence, Ben sighed. "You're right, Abby. I should've noticed. I guess I've been pretty checked out—I'm sorry." His guilt was evident, and Abby empathized with the admission being difficult.

"It's okay," she soothed. "What matters is that we talk now. What do you think would be a fair adjustment so we're both doing our share?" Ben considered it for a moment. "What if I pay an extra hundred for now?" Abby smiled, relieved at the cooperative spirit. "Sounds perfect."

Their tensions melted over a shared dinner. Turned-out problems arose less when faced together respectfully, without blame or deflection. As their friendship was reaffirmed, Ben tried to communicate more attentively. And Abby was grateful for an easy resolution through empathy above all else.

CHAPTER 17

EMOTIONAL INTELLIGENCE IN THE WORKPLACE

"Emotional intelligence is not about avoiding emotions, but about embracing them, understanding their message, and using them to navigate life with wisdom and grace."

-Anonymous

In any environment where people interact closely, having strong emotional intelligence skills is invaluable. The workplace especially requires navigating intricacies between colleagues, managing conflicts respectfully, and maintaining positivity and productivity even under stress. Those able to recognize and understand emotions—in themselves and others—tend to experience much smoother cooperation and success.

Individuals who possess qualities like self-awareness, empathy, impulse control, and motivation are better equipped to deal with interpersonal challenges that inevitably arise during team projects. Rather than reacting strongly to perceived offenses, they can pause to see multiple perspectives and resolve issues constructively before tensions escalate. Such mediation prevents minor frustrations from spiraling into unnecessary distress or toxic drama.

Good emotional reasoning allows reading how certain approaches may affect colleagues to avoid miscommunications, too. Considering words from the recipient's viewpoint engenders compassion and understanding over defensiveness during difficult talks. This, in turn, fosters open communication as people feel heard and respected through change.

Being socially conscious of moods builds trust and camaraderie, so coworkers can bond effectively while still meeting responsibilities. Amid stress, humor, and support boost morale to tackle hurdles as a united group. Leaders, in particular, should exhibit emotional intelligence to lead through inspiration rather than top-down directives alone.

Even technical roles require soft skills. Creatively brainstorming solutions or negotiating deals relies heavily on nuanced social maneuvering. High EQ aids in recognizing when patience or compromise would benefit an outcome over forcefulness. This gains support for efforts through empathy and respect over fear or friction.

In every field, emotional skills smooth over friction within diverse personalities. Appreciating individual quirks forges team spirit to bring out the best in each contributor's strengths. Such harmonious synergy consistently delivers top-tier work no solitary person could match. No metric can outweigh the agility and fulfillment a cohesive, optimism-driven culture offers.

The Problems Posed by Poor Emotional Intelligence

Within any professional environment, a lack of emotional awareness and regulation can lead to a variety of disruptive issues. Interpersonal conflicts may arise more frequently as impatience, defensiveness, or insensitivity are not curbed. Minor disagreements then escalate into prolonged toxic dynamics, wasting productive work hours in the process.

A lack of self-awareness about one's impact also breeds communication breakdowns that confuse or upset colleagues unnecessarily. Behaviors viewed as harmless hyperactivity or bluntness by one may deeply annoy others trying to concentrate, for example. Without perspective-taking, bad habits persist while teamwork suffers.

When issues go unaddressed beneath the surface, tensions inevitably reach a breaking point. As small frustrations pile up without an outlet, previously manageable triggers may erupt disproportionately over minor sparks. Lashing out damages trust built over time through a single impulsive action.

Repairing bonds tested by heated words demands vulnerability, which few feel ready to show at first. Cooler heads must reach out with empathy and remorse, not pride, to begin mending fences. Questions asked respectfully rebuild understanding where defensiveness previously reigned. Compromise and forgiveness let wounds heal through strengthened compassion.

Leaders set the tone for the environment's emotional climate. Those who bristle under strain set examples of reactivity over positivity. As difficult problems arise and creative solutions are needed, directives are shouted down from the above crush initiative. Morale sinks when effort feels underrewarded, besides criticism alone.

Leaders connect with people's spirits to inspire passion for a shared purpose, not just scores or sales. Expressing care for humanity within operations affirms each person's inherent worth beyond metrics. Two-way transparency builds confidence to propose new angles, tried consensually. Outliers accepted broad perspectives to permeate groupthink stagnation.

Though addressing sensitivities exposes vulnerabilities, shielding discomfort enables toxicity's spread instead of solutions. Candid discussions clear misunderstandings to uphold dignity for all while troubleshooting constructively. Accountability improves through calm reason, not the threat of reprisal-fearing openness.

With emotional maturity guiding an organization's culture, even challenging changes feel safe to navigate together. Conflict handled respectfully strengthens the foundations for facing subsequent tests of teamwork and tenacity. Through cooperation, not compliance, any person can achieve shared dreams simply by bringing their best selves as companions on the shared journey.

On all levels, a lack of empathy enables insensitivity, hurt feelings, and disproportionate conflicts originating from minor triggers or slights. Work that should delight then feels draining amid constant relational friction and unaddressed misunderstandings left to fester. No role, project, or vision could thrive without harmony between its human components.

Developing self-awareness and consideration for others creates a more positive workplace focused on solutions rather than cooperation. Constructive attitudes boost both morale and results.

Cultivating Connection Through
Emotional Intelligence at Work

One can use many methods to apply emotional skills helpfully within a professional environment. For oneself, keeping a reflective journal helps increase self-awareness of habitual reactions. Noting triggers, thoughts, and feelings around certain situations provides insight into blind spots. Daily check-ins on mental and emotional wellbeing also boost calm, focus, and care among colleagues.

Communicating considers tone and its potential interpretations carefully. Frames issues around behaviors objectively, not personalities, to resolve rather than attack. Actively listens with compassion through body language, avoiding multitasking disrespectfully. Asking thoughtful questions clarifies intentions nicely compared to accusations.

Conflict mediation looks at all sides with empathy, summarizing each view fairly to find middle-ground solutions agreeably. Compromise validates everyone's perspectives instead of winners and losers. Follow-ups ensure agreements stick through open communication with others.

Leaders motivate authentically by role-modeling balance and resilience. Praise efforts proportionately to encourage positive habits. Criticism focuses constructively on impacts rather than character. Approachable availability promotes safety and allows people to freely share and support each other's well-being.

Where rigidity and conflict hold sway, productivity suffers as defensive energies abound. However, embracing diverse viewpoints as equally valid sparks innovative solutions that surpass any one alone. Flexibility to compromise halfway respects all shadings of an issue and weaves them into strong, nuanced solutions.

Patience allows robust discussion where haste risks misunderstanding. Breathing space clears tensions before deciding critically impacts cooperation. Thoughtfully considering how changes impact various roles keeps everyone invested. This cultivates goodwill where an "my way or the highway" mentality breeds passiveness at best and revolt at worst.

At the same time, thoughtful team-building activities beyond work strengthen familiarity and care between colleagues. Be it casual lunches outside four walls or periodic social gatherings, voluntary fun together lets guards relax among those now friends, not just coworkers. Extended benefits materialize from these bonds under stress, too.

Small gestures like thank-you cards or occasional treats lift morale significantly more than occasional bonuses alone. Feeling appreciated motivates giving one's best, not from orders but from an internal drive to contribute to one's beloved workplace family. This symbiosis inspires revolutionary outcomes beyond any mandated directives.

Prioritizing how policy impacts human relationships above all else transforms an environment from transactional to mission-driven. People invest their whole selves enthusiastically when supported as valued individuals, not replaceable cogs. An empowering, empathetic culture anchored in dignity and goodwill nurtures talent that otherwise might wither without soulfulness.

Under compassionate leadership, even difficult changes feel empowering if included in every step. Mutual understanding and care fuel success where compliance and coercion would splinter resolve. Unity strengthens what any regulation could only hope to constrain as people bring their best selves instead of guarded, performative selves. With emotional skills guiding interactions, no boundaries can contain such a force.

Why Self-Awareness and Relationship Skills Matter

Gaining mastery over one's emotions and social skills reaps wide-ranging advantages, both professionally and personally. On a basic level, self-awareness helps identify internal triggers for certain behaviors and reactions. Understanding why certain issues push personal buttons makes one less prone to knee-jerk responses driven by subconscious biases. This permits pausing to consider multiple viewpoints in difficult discussions rather than reacting strongly.

Such impulse control preserves relationships where hasty retorts may damage them. It also improves work performance by focusing energy constructively despite challenges. Less stressed and defensive, creative problem-solving flourishes. Leaders with self-awareness inspire authentic motivation in others through role-modeling balanced wellness habits. They make wise, inclusive decisions that benefit all parties by understanding different perspectives.

Empathy fuels smoother cooperation in teams by appreciating colleagues as individuals. Despite task demands, maintaining morale and emotional safety invites freely sharing ideas. Conflicts addressed respectfully through open communication deepen trust and engagement between people. As cooperation strengthens, so too do results, making emotional skills a professional asset.

On a mental health level, self-awareness and relationship management alleviate distress. By noting how actions affect others, one can adjust behaviors to minimize friction over time. Resolving issues directly instead of harboring resentment prevents toxic pressures from building internally. Close bonds built on honesty and respect bolster wellbeing, along with a sense of community.

Cultivating emotional intelligence through reflection and conscious interpersonal effort yields growth in many life dimensions. Both career success and quality personal connections rely on effectively applying these "soft" social skills. Overall, well-roundedness and fulfillment follow from developing mastery in both the logical and emotional aspects of living. In a world where we are all interconnected, Emotional Intelligence paves the way to thriving with compassion.

CHAPTER 18

MOTIVATING YOURSELF AND OTHERS

"The greatest discovery of my generation is that a human being can alter his life by altering his attitude."
— William James

Motivation is key to achievement in any endeavor. Whether pursuing a degree, career goals, or hobbies and passions, the drive to continue when faced with obstacles and the desire to improve are crucial. Motivation stems from internal and external factors for students, and looking closely at what inspires you can help catalyze success.

Intrinsically, being interested in your studies and finding personal meaning in the material will light that internal fire to keep learning. If you see the direct value and relevance of your courses to your future plans, you are more likely to dedicate time and effort. Connecting lectures and assignments to real-world applications provides context that transforms abstract concepts into engaging topics. Finding enjoyment and fulfillment through challenging yourself with difficult material also fuels motivation.

Meanwhile, external motivators include goals, recognition, and competition. Having clearly defined objectives for what you want to achieve by completing your degree gives you tangible milestones and a future reward to work towards. Setting deadlines and making plans with friends to study or work on group projects are good ways to accountably structure your time. Earning praise and positive reinforcement from professors and peers when you do well on exams provides encouragement. Competing to get the top grade in a class or for academic awards can also be motivational for some students by satisfying competitive instincts.

Family and community are further external driving forces. Knowing that your education will make your parents proud and help support your family can stimulate diligence in your studies. Feeling part of a university community and its traditions through extracurricular activities fosters a sense of responsibility, commitment, and school spirit. Working towards contributing value to society upon graduation also strengthens resolve.

Naturally, motivation fluctuates depending on individual circumstances and stages of life. Overcoming obstacles is made easier with the right mindset, though. Reframing setbacks and failures as learning experiences will make future success sweeter and help maintain drive even in tougher times. Developing mental habits of self-encouragement and celebrating small wins prevents demoralization. Taking occasional breaks to relax and recharge without feeling guilty is likewise important for long-term motivation.

Sustained motivation ultimately comes from within but can be influenced by one's environment. Finding purpose and meaning in your studies through internal interests while setting achievable external goals with social support systems optimizes conditions for success. With diligent effort and determination to push through challenges, strong motivation is the force that transforms potential into achievement.

Emotional Intelligence and Self-Motivation

Our emotions play a powerful yet often under-acknowledged role in motivation and achievement. Developing emotional intelligence, or the ability to understand and manage feelings, is key to sustaining personal drive long-term. When we listen to our emotions and recognize what inspires versus discourages us, we gain insight into optimizing our mindset and environment for peak performance.

Self-awareness of our emotional states and their causes provides clarity. Are you feeling overwhelmed by piling up too many tasks? Bored by a lack of challenge or interest? Reflecting on the triggers of positive and negative emotions reveals how to recreate and alleviate the former. For instance, breaking up a long study session with a short break boosts energy levels and focus, rather than leading to burnout. Self-monitoring helps channel emotions constructively.

Self-management strengthens willpower during difficulties. We all experience moments of self-doubt, frustration, or lack of motivation when facing academic setbacks or workload stresses. However, those with high emotional intelligence control impulses to procrastinate or give up by redirecting thoughts, utilizing relaxation techniques, or activating support systems. Rather than avoidance, they problem-solve productively through challenges, with resilience fostered by emotional discipline.

Empathy, or understanding others' perspectives and feelings, also plays a role. Cultivating empathy for teachers juggling responsibilities, peers facing their own pressures, or family impacts of one's education engenders patience and compromise during interactions. It reduces conflict and resentment that sap motivation, instead promoting cooperation to overcome hurdles together. Perceived social support itself lifts mood and engagement.

Emotional reasoning observes the link between thoughts, feelings, and behaviors to motivate change. Asking how distress over a bad grade, for instance, impacts study habits, exposes maladaptive patterns,0 and fuels motivation to try new strategies. Positive emotional consequences of practices like consistent preparation keep them ongoing.

Developing emotional intelligence equips one to harness feelings as fuel rather than be controlled by them. By gaining self-awareness, management abilities, empathy, and insight to recognize connections, people motivate themselves sustainably towards continual growth and the achievement of objectives. It is truly a skill that magnifies all others.

The Power of Encouragement: Motivating Others

While the ability to motivate oneself is important for achievement, impacting those around us can be just as meaningful. Research shows that people who feel encouraged and supported by others tend to be more driven, productive, and satisfied with whatever goals or work they pursue. As such, learning the subtle art of encouragement can facilitate motivation for ourselves and those we engage with daily.

One method is simply listening without judgment and reflecting back on what people communicate to feel understood. Validating emotional experiences and viewpoints, even if we disagree, builds rapport where motivation can take root. Offering specific compliments about qualities, efforts, or progress, someone has shown rather than generic praise also empowers motivation by pinpointing strengths. Noting both successes and failures or struggles as learning experiences normalizes setbacks and fuels resilience.

Leading by example as a motivated person inspires others through actions that speak louder than words. Displaying a passion for our own responsibilities and tasks signals their importance, while staying composed during stressful periods models stress management. Ongoing encouragement is most effective when balanced with occasional constructive critique delivered sensitively and paired with suggestions for growth.

Seeing potential in others that they have yet to recognize in themselves broadens perception and boosts confidence, which is central to taking action. Believing in someone's abilities and offering opportunities for new challenges allows capacities to develop fully with room to learn from mistakes. Praising efforts and perseverance as much as or more than results alone keeps motivation thriving even when success is still out of reach.

Leaders who cultivate enthusiasm for a shared mission by clarifying why work matters motivate collectives. Explaining visions and how each role contributes to the purpose lifts group morale and identity. Recognition of teamwork from managers ensures that cooperation is valued more than solely on merit. Togetherness built through informality, celebrations, and perspective-taking between roles motivates ongoing commitment.

In the end, any act reminding another person that they are valued and that their talents or strides forward do not go unnoticed can rekindle motivation or strengthen its steady pace. With tact and authenticity, our encouragement empowers others and enriches our lives through their accomplishments.

The Upsides of Motivation

While motivation requires effort, the inherent rewards it cultivates make that effort well worth it. For students, workers, or anyone pursuing meaningful goals, maintaining drive and focus comes with immense benefits that radiate into all areas of life. In academics, motivated individuals tend to learn more effectively and perform at a higher caliber. Their persistence allows understanding to deepen as challenges are solved and deadlines are consistently met. Overall success and achievement then feed continued progress in a positive cycle.

As discussed previously, motivation is linked to stronger well-being through the encouragement of healthier habits and stress management. Sustaining drive brings clear professional benefits, too, something worth expanding on. When passionate about work, people naturally want to perform their best, take on more responsibility, and find new ways to grow their skills. Bosses tend to notice those who go above and beyond routinely without oversight. Their dependability and high-quality productivity open career doors over the long run that less motivated workers may not access otherwise.

Reliable self-starters tend to be the first to be considered for promotions into leadership roles requiring more independence and critical thinking, as their work can be trusted. Consistently meeting expectations and deadlines without excuses earns raises more swiftly as well. Bosses want to reward those who increase the success of their business or organization through determination and ownership of their duties. A history of solving problems creatively further sets motivated employees apart for exciting new challenges and opportunities to take initiatives to the next level. They become the go-to candidates that employers want on their teams based on a proven drive to deliver results.

At the same time, motivation translates to physical and mental healthcare. Remaining engaged in exercise and other hobbies prevents sedentary lifestyles linked to many illnesses. Regular activity boosts brain function and clarity through heightened blood flow and releases endorphins during and after workouts that improve mood. Difficult yet stimulating work projects paired with meaningful goals that interest someone provide a sense of purpose, keeping the mind and body active. Feelings of progress and success counteract depression, anxiety, and related conditions fueled by boredom or stagnancy.

Viewing obstacles in life or career slumps as temporary problems to overcome rather than insurmountable blocks fosters tenacity in motivated people. They persist in finding solutions rather than dwelling on setbacks that sap morale. A positive mindset that maintains optimism through challenges becomes a self-fulfilling prophecy, enhancing resilience during stressful periods. To sum it up, life satisfaction increases when you continuously work and learn toward important aims. In these ways, motivation enhances more than just professional fortunes by fundamentally supporting well-rounded health.

Relationally, motivation is infectious. Seeking continual improvement as role models motivates friends and family through inspiration. Leading active social lives and taking genuine interest in others fosters strong bonds and support systems that deepen satisfaction from relationships of all kinds. Motivated individuals are more engaged community members, volunteers, and parents who spread drive to causes and future generations.

Developing and sustaining motivation ultimately cultivates successful, fulfilled, and happier lives overall. The self-discipline and routines it builds become daily habits, promoting growth both in capabilities and as people. Its countless upsides make small efforts to find and follow through on purposes well worth any challenge, reaping rewards for years ahead.

CHAPTER 19

OVERCOMING LIMITING BELIEFS

"Emotional intelligence helps us see that limiting beliefs are not truths, but stories we tell ourselves. With awareness, we can rewrite them into narratives of strength and possibility."

-Anonymous

Everyone holds certain convictions and preconceptions about themselves, others, and the world developed since childhood that influence behaviors and opportunities. A crucial early step to maximizing potential is examining where and why we form the daily beliefs that guide decisions and reactions. Often unconsciously, myriad little experiences over time shape what we deem possible or outside the realm of consideration. Tracing these origins allows identifying limiting perspectives and expanding horizons.

From birth, caretakers absorb core beliefs through secure attachments. Loving parents who communicate a child's natural gifts instill self-worth and teach that difficulties can be overcome through hard work and perseverance. Negative home lives may, unfortunately, cause some adults to be disappointed or view the world through a distrusting lens. However, these early influences are not fixed; they can evolve through effort later on.

As we gain independence, peers significantly color our philosophy. Those who bully or reject plant seeds of questioning belonging, whereas accepting friends reinforces that kindness still exists. Later, mentors in school or extracurriculars inspire hope through example or advice. Memorable teachers imprint visions of life paths they insist any student can achieve.

Formative books, movies, and role models continue to widen their conceptions during the years of self-discovery as interests take shape. Exposing oneself to ambitious, generous people through biographies or fiction cultivates role models, proving certain beliefs untrue. Equally, regularly consuming limiting worldviews in entertainment risks normalization.

Eventually, independence brings life tests, shaping beliefs through making choices and facing the consequences. Both achievements and failures during this trial phase shape confidence and risk calculations. With experience, once cemented, assumptions become flexible as realities are embraced.

Self-reflection gives power over beliefs inherited from others through analyzing root causes and reactions tied to them. By catching negative thought patterns, new perspectives can replace restrictive ones to enhance motivation. An openness to growth ensures we believe in possibilities not limited by chance alone.

The Perils of Limiting Beliefs

As discussed, the beliefs we develop over time deeply impact our actions and what we feel capable of achieving. While certain convictions provide stability and direction, limiting beliefs pose real "perils" if left unexamined by imposing artificial ceilings. They breed self-doubt where confidence could thrive and protect the undesirable status quo instead of progress. Recognizing how restricting perspectives form allows challenging their validity and replacing them with empowering mindsets.

Core limitations ingrained from childhood through trauma or lacking role models can become self-fulfilling prophecies without challenge. "I'll never be good at math" convinces someone to shy away from analytical challenges, narrowing career paths. "It's too late to pursue my dreams" justifies resigning from unfulfilling jobs. In both, potential goes untapped by misguided beliefs.

Comparing oneself relentlessly to peers fosters imposter syndrome; valuing achievements as worldly proofs invites depression. Fears of judgment hold many back from opportunities to develop skills and networks. Yet each person's journey is unique; we contain depths rarely plumbed worrying over others' opinions.

Society likewise implants constraints dictating that certain genders excel only in stereotypical domains. Internalizing these through a lack of encouragement neglects passions and attributes. While tradition offers guidance, blindly adopting and limiting mores risks squandering talents.

Failure to expand definitions of success leaves content in mediocrity, chasing only conventional definitions like wealth and fame. Life contains richness in relationships, purpose, and ongoing learning seldom recognized without inspecting preconceptions.

Progress demands confronting beliefs sabotaging growth. With openness and effort, replacing limitations with empowering perspectives and unlocking potential gives us the us the freedom to envision and accomplish goals on our own terms.

Transforming Limiting Beliefs into Empowering Perspectives

Now that we understand how beliefs originate and the perils of limits unconsciously accepted, the work begins to reshape detrimental perspectives. This active process of examining previous assumptions and installing new, positive convictions in their place is how hopeful mindsets supporting achievement are cultivated. With a dedication to challenge inherent but unfounded constraints, people gain control over thought patterns and actions no longer ruled by doubts of the past.

The first step involves acknowledging the existence of restrictive beliefs by noticing counterproductive self-talk. Journaling helps surface the undercurrent of negating voices replying to successes, setbacks, or new chances with excuses limiting risk and growth. Saying limiting statements aloud exposes their absurdity and flimsy rationale, which is too easily accepted without question due to habit.

Next, limiting beliefs must be scrutinized to identify the core fear, assumption, or lack they protect, which no longer serves. Questioning things like "What evidence suggests this thought as truth?" reveals most are based on limited experiences, not facts. Imagining how a supportive friend might dispute the belief helps adopt a kinder inner perspective.

Armed with awareness, believable replacements aligning with goals and talents are deliberately installed. Affirming strengths with statements like "I welcome challenges to learn and improve" or "Every experience develops me" retrains thought patterns. Visualizing ideal scenarios of capabilities unlocked through effort installs hopeful mindsets.

External sources bolster the process through the consumption of uplifting stories, profile resilience, and triumph over doubts. Mentors provide objective guidance and challenge insecurities. Entrusting perceived limits to supportive networks ensures against overthinking alone.

With conscious practice, new beliefs feel genuine through small tests of stretching beyond perceived limits safely. As confidence to define one's own potential grows, so does motivation to work toward a self-determined vision of success focused on ongoing learning versus worry over others. Freedom from the cautious scripts of the past emerges through the transformation of once-limiting perspectives.

Many people go through life with negative thought patterns that hold them back from achieving goals and experiencing happiness. However, research shows that maintaining an optimistic mindset can have significant advantages for our well-being and success. This article will explore how adopting positive beliefs about ourselves and our future can empower us to accomplish more.

One key way that optimism is beneficial is by influencing our motivation. When we tell ourselves that things will likely turn out well, it boosts our drive to pursue opportunities and overcome setbacks. Positive thinking helps us persevere through challenges instead of giving up. In contrast, pessimism can be self-fulfilling, as doubting our abilities might cause us to quit early on. Maintaining hope even during difficult periods requires us to work hard for the desired results.

Optimism also enhances our health. Studies have linked a glass half-full attitude to less stress, better cardiovascular function, and a stronger immune system. Our minds directly impact our physical states, so viewing life as generally good rather than threatening puts less strain on the body. Instead of worrying about potential issues, optimists focus mental energy on solutions and daily pleasures that lift the mood. Their resilient nature may help ward off depression and other illnesses over the long term as well.

Relationships benefit as optimists bring out the best in others. Rather than complaining or criticizing, they have constructive conversations and offer encouragement. As a result, optimistic spouses, friends, and coworkers support each other well and create more positive interactions. At work, this mentality fosters collaboration, where people feel motivated to cooperate instead of competing unconstructively. Individuals high in hope also report more satisfying social connections overall.

In academics and career pursuits, maintaining a hopeful outlook pays off. When facing academic challenges, optimistic students persevere with confidence, knowing they have the skills to succeed on their own terms. They stay engaged in class without negatively comparing themselves to others. Similarly, optimists in the workforce handle setbacks, believing they will eventually find solutions or alternative opportunities. This aids professional growth over the long haul, versus blaming external factors for every difficulty. Optimism simply creates a self-reinforcing cycle for achievement.

While optimism cannot solve all of life's problems alone, its many psychological and physical advantages are scientifically proven. Small daily habits like acknowledging progress made rather than focusing on unfinished tasks, expressing gratitude for positives in our lives, or visualizing successful outcomes as motivational goals can nurture a natural optimistic mindset.

Adopting this empowering perspective does not require changing difficult circumstances; it allows us to change how we view and respond to circumstances for increased well-being and success in all areas of life. An optimistic attitude truly has the power to transform one's experiences.

In summary, optimism should be recognized as a vital asset that benefits mental health, physical health, social connections, and goal achievement. Maintaining hope even through difficulties enables perseverance, proactive problem-solving, and building others up. Both research and everyday evidence indicate that fostering a positive outlook through conscious practice can significantly improve the quality of life overall. While external factors influence us, optimism ultimately comes down to an internal choice of how we explain events and envision our futures.

Many people go through life with negative thought patterns that hold them back from achieving goals and experiencing happiness. However, research shows that maintaining an optimistic mindset can have significant advantages for our well-being and success. This article will explore how adopting positive beliefs about ourselves and our future can empower us to accomplish more.

One key way that optimism is beneficial is by influencing our motivation. When we tell ourselves that things will likely turn out well, it boosts our drive to pursue opportunities and overcome setbacks. Positive thinking helps us persevere through challenges instead of giving up. In contrast, pessimism can be self-fulfilling, as doubting our abilities might cause us to quit early on. Maintaining hope even during difficult periods pushes us to work hard for the desired results.

Optimism also enhances our health. Studies have linked a glass half-full attitude to less stress, better cardiovascular function, and a stronger immune system. Our minds directly impact our physical states, so viewing life as generally good rather than threatening puts less strain on the body. Instead of worrying about potential issues, optimists focus mental energy on solutions and daily pleasures that lift the mood. Their resilient nature may help ward off depression and other illnesses over the long term as well.

Relationships benefit as optimists bring out the best in others. Rather than complaining or criticizing, they have constructive conversations and offer encouragement. As a result, optimistic spouses, friends, and coworkers support each other well and create more positive interactions. This mentality fosters collaboration at work, where people feel motivated to cooperate instead of competing unconstructively. Individuals high in hope also report more satisfying social connections overall.

In academics and career pursuits, maintaining a hopeful outlook pays off. When facing academic challenges, optimistic students persevere with confidence, knowing they have the skills to succeed on their own terms. They stay engaged in class without negatively comparing themselves to others. Similarly, optimists in the workforce handle setbacks, believing they will eventually find solutions or alternative opportunities. This aids professional growth over the long haul, versus blaming external factors for every difficulty. Optimism simply creates a self-reinforcing cycle for achievement.

While optimism cannot solve all of life's problems alone, its many psychological and physical advantages are scientifically proven. Small daily habits like acknowledging progress made rather than focusing on unfinished tasks, expressing gratitude for positives in our lives, or visualizing successful outcomes toward motivational goals can nurture a natural optimistic mindset. Adopting this empowering perspective does not require changing difficult circumstances; it allows us to change how we view and respond to circumstances for increased well-being and success in all areas of life. An optimistic attitude truly has the power to transform one's experiences.

Optimism should be recognized as a vital asset that benefits mental health, physical health, social connections, and goal achievement. Maintaining hope even through difficulties enables perseverance, proactive problem-solving, and building others up. Both research and everyday evidence indicate that fostering a positive outlook through conscious practice can significantly improve the quality of life overall. While external factors influence us, optimism ultimately comes down to an internal choice of how we explain events and envision our futures.

CHAPTER 20

APPLYING EMOTIONAL INTELLIGENCE IN EVERYDAY LIFE

"Emotional intelligence is the ability to be aware of our own emotions and the emotions of others, and to use that awareness to manage ourselves and our relationships more effectively."

-Anonymous

As we are moving closer to the end of our journey together, I want to remind the readers that it's important to take time each day to focus on our emotional well-being. How we process and understand our emotions greatly impacts our stress levels, relationships, and overall happiness. When we can identify how we're feeling and why, it's easier to manage difficult emotions in a healthy way. It also allows us to have more compassion for others.

We can do a few key things to improve our emotional intelligence. First, check in with yourself regularly to notice any changes in your mood, energy levels, or behavior. Pay attention to the little cues your body gives you about your feelings. Writing things down can help you better analyze patterns.

Next, try putting yourself in someone else's shoes when dealing with a conflict or disagreement. Don't just assume you know why they said what they said or did what they did. Ask questions to understand their perspective. In most cases, there are multiple sides to every story. Empathy and the ability to see gray areas are important for building strong relationships.

It's also important that we manage our own emotions effectively. When feeling upset, take some deep breaths before responding. Count to 10 if needed. Removing yourself from the situation for a bit can also help you gain some clarity and objectivity. Try expressing your feelings using "I feel..." statements instead of accusations like "you always..."

And don't forget to have self-compassion. We all make mistakes or say things we regret sometimes when our emotions are high. Forgive yourself and others. Beating yourself up adds unnecessary stress and gets in the way of growth. Looking at challenges as learning experiences instead of failures is a sign of strong emotional maturity.

At school or in the workplace, emotional intelligence plays a key role in how well you can communicate, collaborate with others, and handle stressful events. Learning to recognize nonverbal cues like body language and tone of voice gives you important social information beyond what someone is just saying with words. It makes you a caring listener and helps build trust.

Use your emotional skills to motivate and energize yourself as well. Notice what inspires you or helps lift your mood on difficult days. Make time for enjoyable activities that relax your mind and body. Your passions and interests outside of studies or careers can recharge you mentally and physically. Balance is very important.

Managing emotions is a lifelong journey that takes regular effort and practice. However, being more self-aware and developing a deep understanding of others will enrich your relationships and how you experience life overall. By caring for your emotional well-being each day, even in small ways, you cultivate a skill that makes you wiser, happier, and more compassionate.

Overcoming Hurdles in Our Daily Lives

"Change is the end result of all true learning."
— Leo Buscaglia

We all face big and small challenges in our everyday routines. It can be easy to feel overwhelmed by things that don't always go according to plan. However, learning to roll with life's imperfections in a flexible way is so important for our mental well-being and happiness. While problems are inevitable, how we choose to deal with them makes all the difference.

Something as minor as waking up late and rushing out the door can start our day off on the wrong foot if we let little frustrations get to us. But we have a choice: do we panic and stress or take a breath and shift our mindset? Most of the time, things work out just fine, even if they're not ideal. And looking at inconveniences as temporary bumps rather than catastrophic issues provides so much relief.

Keeping a productive schedule while balancing other commitments like family, chores, friends, and self-care isn't always straightforward either. Unexpected events will cause schedule changes, and that's okay. We have to be gentle with ourselves on imperfect days. Maybe one task gets postponed, or another gets low priority - as long as we don't lose sight of our goals overall.

Interpersonal conflicts or misunderstandings can also disrupt our mood yet remain completely out of control. Instead of fueling annoyance, think about constructive solutions and try seeing another point of view. We all make mistakes in relationships sometimes. Whether others forgive us or we forgive them, the ability to forgive lifts a huge mental weight.

Nobody has life completely figured out. Showing up for ourselves through unpredictable seasons and lacking motivation or momentum requires patience and self-encouragement. These phases don't last. Trust that challenges are just part of life's natural ups and downs, not signs that anything is wrong with us. Have faith in your resilience.

By acknowledging that little problems don't define us but are normal human experiences, we gain freedom from their power to ruin our days. Circumstances ebb and flow. Our well-being depends far more on how we frame inconveniences than on avoiding them completely. With life's imperfections comes beauty, too, when we stay centered.

Emotional Intelligence in Everyday Moments

It's easy to go through our daily routines on autopilot without consciously applying emotional intelligence skills. But making small adjustments can have big impacts on our stress levels, relationships, and how much we appreciate life's little moments. Our emotions influence so much of what we say and do, whether we realize it or not. We cultivate greater well-being by bringing more awareness, compassion, and self-control into our everyday interactions.

Noticing how we feel physically can help us quickly understand what might be bothering us emotionally under the surface. Even small hints like tension or butterflies could indicate needing to slow down, take space if upset, or reconnect with people who energize us. Checking in regularly, like journaling feelings, ensures we don't ignore our body's cues until things spiral.

Managing Emotions in Everyday Interactions

"Emotional intelligence is the key to both personal and professional success."

— Daniel Goleman

Our daily lives present countless opportunities to interact with others, from casual greetings to deeper conversations. How we navigate these exchanges impacts relationships as well as our own well-being. However, utilizing skills like active listening, expressing care, and resolving conflicts respectfully doesn't always come naturally. It requires awareness and practice.

When frustrations arise, our initial instinct may be to lash out or shut down. But these knee-jerk reactions often do more harm than good. By collecting our thoughts before responding, space is created for understanding rather than accusation. Simply removing ourselves from the situation for a bit if we are very upset allows emotions to calm so we can approach issues thoughtfully.

Deep breathing is a powerful way to diffuse tension in the body when feelings run high. Inhaling and exhaling slowly with intention shifts us out of "fight or flight" mode into a more relaxed state. From that grounded place, it becomes easier to communicate compassionately rather than reactively blaming others. Using "I feel" statements also prevents them from feeling attacked directly while still being open about how the situation affects them.

The Power of Active Listening and
Small Acts of Kindness

Our daily interactions provide endless opportunities to either strengthen bonds or cause divisions. However, utilizing simple skills like active listening and showing care for others can transform surface-level exchanges into meaningful connections. Making a genuine effort to understand different perspectives and spread goodwill goes a long way toward building rapport.

When disagreements happen, the natural instinct is to defend our viewpoints right away. But pausing to first hear the other side fully, without judgment, and with an open mind, allows deeper understanding beyond initial reactions. Asking respectful questions for clarity and summarizing what we heard ensures we properly grasp their experience before responding. This approach prevents conflicts from escalating due to issues like crossed signals.

Body language and subtle vocal cues also provide important context outside of straight words. All their forms of expression are taken in when they are intently focused on others as they converse. This allows us to see multiple layers of complexity within situations rather than oversimplifying from a single angle. People feel truly listened to when they have our complete presence, free of distractions like phones or technology.

Active listening like this fosters an environment where all feel truly valued and encouraged to open up freely. It says, "I'm here for you," rather than jumping ahead to reply first. As a result, relationships strengthen through genuine knowing of one another built over time in everyday exchanges rather than just superficiality. This level of care and understanding moves groups towards more compassionate and solution-based interactions overall.

Beyond words, small acts show that we notice others making positive ripples, too. A sincere smile acknowledges human worth beyond superficial characteristics alone. Noting something specific we appreciate about acquaintances, from styling a hijab beautifully to recently completing a degree program, taps into the best of human nature through compliments. People light up when they feel seen for who they are.

Little efforts, like maintaining eye contact in conversations or asking about someone's day, indicate our presence and interest in their lives. Writing heartfelt thank you cards highlights how contributions matter. Acts of service through volunteering or meals for grieving families strengthen communal ties more than fleeting "likes" online ever could. Together, these empathetic gestures form strong foundations of trust and goodwill as we walk alongside one another.

We avoid unnecessary stress and hurt feelings by practicing emotional awareness and compassion, even in mundane interactions. It also strengthens bonds that enhance our experience of moving through life together. Handling exchanges thoughtfully becomes increasingly natural with effort over time.

Noting what inspires us each day fuels ongoing motivation despite challenges. While daily tasks might drag, immersing in a hobby, appreciating art, or trying new recipes brings moments of presentness and clarity. Caring for our minds through learning something uplifting prevents autopilot negativity.

We avoid harsh self-criticism that creates unneeded pressure by choosing compassion for ourselves, even in times of self-doubt or busyness. Self-care and balance energize us to show up fully present wherever our paths lead each day.

CHAPTER 21

THE JOURNEY AHEAD-
CONTINUING TO GROW
AND EVOLVE

"Watch your thoughts, they become words; watch your words, they become actions; watch your actions, they become habits; watch your habits, they become character; watch your character, for it becomes your destiny."

—Frank Outlaw

As we near the close of our exploration into emotional intelligence, taking time to reflect on all that's been covered seems fitting. From the beginning, our goal has been to better understand this concept and how applying certain skills can create positive change. Now seems like the right moment to reconnect the pieces by reviewing the core ideas and their interlinking nature.

We started by discussing what emotional intelligence entails—the ability to recognize our own emotions and those of others and how to manage strong reactions in productive ways. This allows for healthier relationships defined by empathy, compassion, and effective problem-solving rather than conflict. The importance of self-awareness through checking in regularly on feelings came next, including journaling for patterns.

Throughout the initial chapters, gaining relevant perspective has proven key, whether through envisioning others' viewpoints during disagreements, acknowledging life's imperfections gracefully, or noticing what inspires gratitude each day. Developing empathy and handling conflicts respectfully fortifies bonds of trust. Pausing to listen fully without judgment fosters an environment for understanding over superficial interactions alone.

While following a progressive pattern, an individual can work on emotional skills like these, which take practice yet nurture personal and communal well-being. While stressful situations remain inevitable, cultivating humility, forgiveness, and patience lightens burdens to endure. Making compassion a priority, even for oneself amid self-doubt, avoids unnecessary pressure through harsh self-talk.

Connecting everything covered gives us a holistic picture of how tending to emotions significantly shapes life experience. Small, conscious choices each day compound significantly over time. Approaching relationships and difficulties with presence, flexibility, and care rather than reactivity cultivates inner strength and healthier communities. May these refreshed understandings continue to empower positive change.

If we trace back to where the idea of emotional intelligence first emerged, it was through the work of psychologists in the 1980s and 1990s who began researching this concept. They noticed that IQ and academic skills alone don't determine life success; other personal attributes play a huge role, too. Being self-aware, managing distressing emotions well, and having empathy are vital skills for mental well-being and navigating relationships.

This led to the term "emotional intelligence" being coined to describe an array of abilities distinct from but just as important as intellectual capabilities. It refers to how well we understand ourselves, connect with others, and handle challenges and conflicts. Two main researchers who explored this topic early on were Peter Salovey from Yale University and John Mayer from the University of New Hampshire. Their work shed light on EI as a new framework for examining personality.

Meanwhile, during the 1990s, psychologist Daniel Goleman took these early social and emotional competence theories and brought them to mainstream attention through books like "Emotional Intelligence." He highlighted research demonstrating how EQ plays a greater role in career success and quality of life than IQ alone. Things like the ability to motivate oneself, show empathy, and soothe anxieties in relationships heavily influence well-being and performance.

Goleman's studies demonstrated that these social-emotional skills could be learned at any stage. This was welcomed news at a time when intellect on its own was seen as fixed by adulthood. He urged focus on strengthening abilities like self-awareness, self-management, social awareness, and relationship management to benefit both personal and professional lives. His writing helped validate emotional skills as key areas for development, not just intellectual ones.

Since then, more models of EI have been proposed, along with various tools to assess and measure these abilities. However, at its core, most definitions agree that it involves a set of personal and interpersonal competencies related to identifying emotions, using them to make decisions, and handling relationships to enhance living. These remain as relevant today as when the concept was originally explored, shedding light on the multi-dimensional nature of intelligence beyond academics alone.

The Building Blocks of Emotional Intelligence

Now that we've reviewed the origins of emotional intelligence, let's examine its key components in more depth. Most researchers agree that EI comprises four core abilities that work together to enhance how we navigate life and relationships. Developing skills in each area cultivates greater well-being for ourselves and others.

Self-awareness involves closely examining one's own emotions, strengths and weaknesses, values, and impact on others. This enables an understanding of internal states and triggers. It is recognizing how outside events make us feel physically and mentally and learning more about who we are. Self-aware people can identify feelings and use them to guide their thinking productively.

Self-regulation connects to self-awareness through careful monitoring of emotions. It's utilizing techniques to stay flexible and optimistic when facing challenges. Tactics like relaxation, reappraising situations positively, and not overreacting keep us interacting helpfully instead of destructively when distressed. Strong self-regulators remain calm, clear-headed, and open under pressure.

Empathy acts as the social awareness component through perspective-taking. It's understanding others' viewpoints by paying attention to nonverbal emotional cues and actively envisioning their experiences. This lets us exhibit compassion through respectful listening and acknowledging different feelings without judgment. Empathetic people form deeper connections.

Relationship management skills rely on self-awareness, self-regulation, and empathy. It handles interpersonal interactions smoothly by clearly communicating, resolving conflicts fairly, and motivating cooperation. Good relationship skills inspire trust through qualities like warmth, honesty, and responding sensitively to group dynamics.

Our well-being and performance can take significant shifts towards progression by incorporating the EI skillset. While a lifelong journey, conscious practice can significantly strengthen social-emotional development at any stage of life.

Understanding Emotions and the Value of Social Awareness

A key component in developing emotional intelligence involves understanding both our own emotions and those of others. This ability relies heavily on social awareness, which is an important skill to cultivate through interaction and observation. Identifying what various feelings look and feel like allows us to thoughtfully navigate relationships.

While some emotions, like happiness or anger, come with fairly clear physical signs, others are more subtle. Taking time each day to tune into what's happening inside and asking how external events make us feel physically helps build self-awareness. Noting patterns of when we feel tension, excitement, or other sensations provides valuable self-knowledge that aids in interacting constructively.

Just as important as recognizing internal states is comprehending those around us through perspective-taking. Truly grasping another viewpoint requires empathy. This involves gathering context through both verbal and nonverbal communication to accurately read situations. Social cues like tone of voice, facial expressions, and body language all convey important emotional data beyond mere words.

Reading further, paying close attention to such signals during group interactions highlights our impact on others while also providing insight into developing dynamics. Making eye contact, orienting our body toward the speaker, and asking follow-up questions allow deeper listening and empathy. Making an effort to understand complex emotional realities enriches our relationships.

Awareness equally applies to larger social environments. Keeping an open, non-judgmental perspective regarding different cultural norms and experiences promotes compassion. Valuing diversity within communities prevents leaning too heavily on one worldview alone. This appreciation of multiple realities strengthens the greater whole through respectful cooperation and by addressing all needs.

We can develop abilities to recognize emotions thoughtfully, whether personally or that of others, creating a foundation for positively navigating life together. While a continued practice, conscious focus on such social-emotional learning reaps rewards well beyond childhood into adulthood through healthy relationships and well-being.

Key Social-Emotional Skills for Strengthening Well-Being

Earlier, we reviewed the components that make up emotional intelligence and their importance. Now let's explore some specific techniques that fall under these pillars, which we can actively practice to build greater EI over time. Developing a "toolkit" of skills supports well-being through challenging periods as well as everyday moments.

Initially, we can recognize our emotions accurately and thoughtfully, which is essential. Designating times like journaling to check in on inner states through body sensations prevents overlooking subtler feelings. This awareness helps manage reactions constructively through techniques like deep breathing, expressing thoughts and feelings rather than bottling them up, and reframing stressful triggers positively.

Equally key is developing empathy—imagining life from others' perspectives, especially during conflicts or misunderstandings. Making space for different viewpoints requires putting judgments aside and listening without interruption or preconceived notions until one fully understands the other. Expressing care and compassion fosters healthy bonds.

Emotional regulation involves techniques that maintain flexibility and optimism while still authentically addressing problems. Skills like compromise, cooling off before responding rationally when heated, and acknowledging imperfections reasonably rather than criticizing productively resolve issues. Responding assertively and calmly sets a tone for cooperation.

Self-confidence stems from self-awareness and care. Self-talk shifting assumptions like "always failing" to compassion helps lift self-doubt. Pursuing interests with grace despite mistakes and celebrating achievements normally overlooked instead of perfectionism fosters inner strength. Seeing ourselves and others empathetically cultivates well-being.

With practice, these social-emotional techniques become increasingly natural, even in challenging circumstances. Combined, they nurture the pillars of EI behind healthy relationships, resilience, and life satisfaction over the long term. Making progress feels uplifting, no matter where one is on the journey.

Enhancing Well-Being Through Social-Emotional Skills

Strong social skills allow us to meaningfully connect with others. Actively listening without distractions, initiating conversations with interest by asking about people's lives, and resolving conflicts respectfully are foundations. Communicating effectively builds on these strengths through clearly expressing needs and thoughts, seeking common ground constructively in disagreements, and understanding different personalities.

One can cultivate resilience by guarding against life's difficulties and embracing learning from challenges along the way. A positive outlook empowering perseverance through setbacks, flexibility adapting to changes smoothly, and self-care recharging us for what's ahead bolsters coping abilities. Handling stress relies on these supports as well. Techniques like deep breathing, conscious optimism, balancing responsibilities, and outlets like exercise ease pressure and prevent weariness.

Overall, regularly practicing an array of social-emotional skills like perspective-taking, emotional regulation, compassion, and empathy lays a strong foundation for well-being. While naturally strengthening over time, making space to focus on interactions thoughtfully and with presence enriches relationships and endurance in handling difficulties. However the journey unfolds, these techniques can smooth paths and add depth to everyday life when obstacles arise. Our quality of life stems greatly from how we engage within the community.

Emotional Intelligence in Building Connections

Navigating diverse viewpoints respectfully takes practice. Active listening without judgment helps resolve conflicts cooperatively. As leaders, showing compassion encourages openness, while addressing misunderstandings constructively sets examples.

Relationships similarly require empathy, care, and flexibility on an ongoing basis. Appreciating another's perspective alongside one's own nurtures understanding during disagreements or changes. Expressing care for someone's overall well-being, not just resolving single issues, strengthens reliability within connections.

Even difficult conversations become manageable, focusing on shared hopes instead of past problems alone. When tensions arise, solutions emerge through patience and emotional control, favoring rapport over winning arguments. Recognizing imperfections on all sides promotes forgiveness and moving forward positively.

Emotionally intelligent skills like cooperation, emotional regulation, and perspective-taking facilitate smooth personal and professional interactions. While continuously developing with life changes, consciously applying such competencies sustains healthy cooperation and bonds crucial for wellness in communities.

Applying Emotional Intelligence at Work and in Daily Life

Emotional intelligence skills are invaluable not just for relationships but also for navigating professional demands and routine moments. Social competencies like self-awareness, communication, and conflict management foster productivity within diverse teams striving for common goals in the workplace.

Self-motivation energizes endeavors through uplifting self-talk and embracing imperfect progress. Having empathy for colleagues' experiences and viewpoints creates an encouraging environment where everyone's talents feel valued. Flexibility in adapting to changing needs reduces undue stress, allowing creativity to flow. Networking relies on social skills like active listening and relationship-building through sincerity. Overcoming limiting self-beliefs with patience maximizes opportunities; we all continue growing regardless of past experiences. Providing support and meaningful feedback strengthens morale.

In daily life, too, a toolkit of EI techniques enhances well-being. From perceiving emotions accurately to then asserting perspectives calmly, these skills make even chores or errands more manageable. Expressing care through small acts and appreciation lightens social interactions.

Whether at work, home, or beyond, consciously focusing on interactions and ourselves yields lasting benefits. Regularly practicing competencies like emotional regulation, resilience-building, cooperation, and self-awareness nurtures deeper satisfaction from life's routines as well as complexities through a foundation of empathy, care, and personal and interpersonal growth.

REFERENCES

Brown, B. (2012). *Daring greatly: How the courage to be vulnerable transforms the way we live, love, parent, and lead. Gotham Books.*

Bucaglia, L. (n.d.). *Change is the end result of all true learning.*

Frank, V. E. (2006) *Man's search for meaning. Beacon Press.*

Goleman, D. (1995). *Emotional intelligence: Why it can matter more than IQ. Bantam Books.*

James, W. (n.d.). *The greatest discovery of my generation is that a human being can alter his life by altering his attitudes.*

Miller, A. (2013). *The drama of the gifted child: The search for the true self. Basic Books.*

Narcissistic Abuse Recovery. (n.d.). *Understanding narcissistic abuse and recovery. Retrieved from Narcissistic Abuse Recovery.*

Rosenberg, M. B. (2003). *Nonviolent communication: A language of life. PuddleDancer Press.*

Smith, M. (2016). *The art of difficult conversations: How to talk about what matters most. Harvard Business Review Press.*

Stone, D., Patton, B., & Heen, S. (2010). *Difficult conversations: How to discuss what matters most. Penguin Books.*

Tannen, D. (2001). *You just don't understand: Women and men in conversation*. HarperCollins.

Walker, L. E. (1997). *The battered woman syndrome*. Springer Publishing Company.

Williams, J. (2017). The need for empathy in difficult conversations: Strategies for improving communication. *Journal of Communication Studies*, 14(2), 45-60.

Salovey, P., & Mayer, J. D. (1990). Emotional intelligence. *Imagination, Cognition and Personality*, 9(3), 185-211. https://doi.org/10.2190/DUGG-P24E-52WK-6E16

Printed in the United States
by Baker & Taylor Publisher Services